Craig Stadler's Complete Golf Desk Reference

TRIUMPH
B O O K S
CHICAGO

Harley Publishing Inc.
Mississauga, Ontario
Canada

Developed by:
Harley Publishing Inc.
1012 Willowbank Trail
Mississauga, Ontario
Canada L4W 3T9

Library of Congress Control Number: 2003116432

This book is available at special discounts for your group or organization.
For more information, contact:

Triumph Books
601 South LaSalle St., Suite 500
Chicago, Illinois 60605
Telephone: (312) 939-3330
Fax: (312) 663-3557

ISBN: 1-57243-621-2

Printed in China

Illustrations: © 2000 Barry Ross
Front Cover Photo: © AP/Wide World Photos
Co-Author: Wayne Nodwell
Designer: Scott McMann
Course Photos: Courtesy of ClubCorp Resorts
Cover Design: Patricia Frey

About the Author

There is no better spokesperson for the everyday golfer than Craig Stadler. Affectionately known as the Walrus, he's as thick in the waist as in the shoulder, grumbles, forgets to comb his hair, and tosses the occasional club when a shot doesn't quite work out. Sound familiar? Yet there's nothing common about his winning the '71 World Junior Championship, the '73 U.S. Amateur Championship, or the '82 Masters. The Walrus has 13 PGA Tour wins and more than $9 million in PGA earnings. Over the past 25 years, Craig's motto has been 'Play golf for enjoyment'. He has also spent considerable time helping less-gifted golfers improve their games by teaching and contributing articles to leading golf publications, which is why he has written the Golf Guide and dedicated it to 'the rest of us'.

Career Highlights	
1971	World Junior Champion
1973	U.S. Amateur Champion
1974-75	All American
1975	Walker Cup Team Member
1980	Bob Hope Desert Classic
	Greater Greensboro Open
1981	Kemper Open
1982	The Masters
	Tucson Open
	Kemper Open
	World Series of Golf
	PGA Tour Leading Money Winner
1983	U.S. Ryder Cup Team
1984	Byron Nelson Classic
1985	U.S. Ryder Cup Team
	European Masters
1987	Dunlop Phoenix
1988	Fred Meyer Challenge *(with Joey Sindelar)*
1990	Scandinavian Enterprise Open
1991	Tour Championship
1992	NEC World Series of Golf
	Argentina Open
1994	Buick Invitational
1995	Hyundai Motor Golf Classic *(with Steve Pate)*
1996	Nissan Open
2003	B.C. Open
	Senior Players Championship (Legends Tour)
	Greater Hickory Classic (Legends Tour)
	SBC Championship (Legends Tour)

Acknowledgments

The idea for this book started with a meeting between Lynn Roach, my manager, and Wayne "Harley" Nodwell, owner of Harley Publishing Inc. Wayne came to Lynn with a concept for a golf instructional and reference book that was unique from other golf texts. It allowed golfers to access help instantly using a series of indexes keyed to each section of the book. Being an avid golfer himself, Wayne felt that there was very little opportunity for accessible instruction for the twenty million golf enthusiasts who play public courses. The book would help fulfill that need.

The concept appealed to me tremendously. From my earliest days of entering peewee events around San Diego, I read everything I could get my hands on to help me develop my game. I would clip articles from golf magazines and make notes that I would 'file' in the bottom of my carry bag or bedroom floor. My mother added to the collection and became an even more avid 'clipper' of articles. Inevitably, the material would disappear and much of the instruction that helped form my game faded from memory.

I decided to undertake the project to provide all golf enthusiasts with hundreds of tips and pointers to improve their understanding and enjoyment of the game.

I would like to thank Lynn Roach and Wayne Nodwell for the concept and support.

A special thanks to Scott White and Rick Watson who encouraged the book's initial publication.

I would also like to acknowledge Mark Russell, a PGA Tour rules official who reviewed and contributed to the section dealing with rules violations. Also, thanks to Neil Yack, associate golf professional at the Mandarin Golf Club in Toronto, and David Clark, currently with the Olympic Club of San Francisco.

Grateful appreciation to Barry Ross, a regular contributor to *Golf Magazine*'s Private Lessons, who provided the wonderful illustrations throughout the book, and Scott McMann for the book's graphic design.

Last but not least, I would like to thank the individuals who convinced me that a rules section was needed and gave their time and permission to be illustrated in the book. A special thanks to Kristin Nodwell, Neil Hutton, Andy Barteaux, Rolly Colvin, Richard Harrison, Peter McBurney, Bob Hall, Jim Gordon, John Glendinning, and Peter Turner.

**Dedicated to everyone
who loves the game.**

Craig Stadler's **Golf Guide** is a 180-page golf instructional and reference book. Unlike most other golf texts, the **Golf Guide** is designed to be used as an 'instant' reference. Its format is 'problem' or 'situation' oriented. The guide incorporates hundreds of ideas and tips aimed at assisting golfers of all levels improve their game.

The format of the guide is unique. Unlike other golf instructional texts, the **Golf Guide** incorporates a revolutionary **'instant-index'** at the center of the book that allows quick access to any section of the text. **No other golf instructional book incorporates this handy 'instant index'.**

Each topic is written in a **clear, concise** manner, **with illustration opposite each page of golf instructional text.** Major sections of the guide cover the following topics.

1. **Swing Basics**
2. **Common Problems and Their Cures**
3. **Positive Putting**
4. **Problem Situations**
5. **Shotmaking**
6. **Reference Charts**
7. **Common Rules Violations**
8. **Games**

Craig Stadler's Golf Guide overcomes the shortcomings of traditional golf instruction books by providing concise, instantly accessible information for serious golfers.

Complementing the **'Instant Index'** at the center of the guide are the **Games Index** near the front of the book and the **Rules Violation Index** in the back portion. Familiarize yourself with the contents of each of the index pages. Flip forward or backwards through the guide using the handy color-coded tabs to find the section you are looking for.

Key Benefits

1. The key to the appeal of this guide is the *'instant index'* feature.
   This allows instant access to the specific problem or situation facing the golfer.

2. The guide is an ideal reference source for the putting green, driving range, or course during practice rounds.

3. The guide is *practical, concise,* and *simple.* It condenses information from many standard texts and puts it into a workable format.

4. The guide is *'problem' or 'situation' oriented.* Each section follows a standard format of description, causes, cures, and practice pointers.

5. The guide is also a *reference book,* summarizing course etiquette and common rules violations.

6. Look for the *Walrus logo* for a quick tip summary at the end of most instruction sections.

The 9th hole, Fazio Foothills,
Barton Creek, TX

Games Index

Old Course, The Homestead, VA

Popular foursome games

1 | Nassau

Nassau is undoubtedly the most popular game in golf. The game is usually played in a match format, although Nassaus can be played in stroke-play format as well.

Nassau is a ***three-point game,*** with one point being awarded for winning the front nine, one point for the second nine, and one (or two) point(s) for the overall eighteen.

The point or value of each side is agreed to before play begins.

Nassaus can be played between two individual players or as team play in a foursome.

There are a number of variations to the standard Nassau.

- Many players like to put a ***higher point value on the full eighteen.*** For example, if the front and back nines are played for one point each, the eighteen hole match would be played for two points.

- Usually, tied holes are thrown out. However, one variation of the standard Nassau is to ***'push' tied holes*** similar to the popular televised Skins Game. For example, if three holes are tied, and a player or team wins the fourth, all four holes are awarded.

- Presses are an important variation to the standard Nassau. (see section 18 in the games index)

2 | Skins

Skins, also known as ***Cats and Skats,*** is an exciting game made popular by NBC Sports telecasts. It can be played with two, three, or four players.

Each hole (or skin) is assigned a point value. Some play the game with a higher value for par 5's and a lesser value for par 3's.

A player wins a skin if he or she wins the hole outright. In the case of a tie for low ball, the skin is carried over to the next hole. Players are handicapped off the golfer with the lowest handicap.

An interesting variation of the game is to double the value of the skin when won with a birdie (including carryovers!)

3 | Low Ball or Low Ball/Low Total

Low ball is one of the simplest games in golf. It can be played in a two golfer match or a foursome.

Players agree on the value of each point before the match.

If a player has the lowest score on a hole, he or she is awarded one point. Points are added at the end of the match.

Low ball/low total is a variation in foursome play. ***Two points are awarded on each hole, one point for low ball and one point for low total for the partners with the lowest aggregate total on each hole.***

Players play off the lowest handicap golfer.

Popular foursome games

4 Round Robins

Also known as **Robins or Hollywoods,** this foursome game is one of golf's most popular. It is ideal for groups of different natural playing abilities since each player is paired at some point in the match with every other player.

The game consists of three 6-hole matches. Partners are chosen by tossing balls on the first tee or by pairing the longest and shortest drives. On the seventh and thirteenth hole the partners switch so that each player is teamed up with the other members of the group at some point in the game.

Points are won by the team with low ball and/or low total for the two partners.

A common variation is to award a point to team B if a player on team A has the high score on a hole.

To add a little excitement, some parts of the country play a 'blind' robin where partners are not picked until the 19th hole.

5 Scotch

Known alternately as **Five Points or Chicago,** Scotch is a **five point per hole game** with a number of possible variations.

- **Two points for low ball**
- **One point for low total**
- **One point for natural birdies**
- **One point for 'greenies'**

'Greenies' are awarded to the player who **hits the green in regulation and is closest to the hole.** Some play a variation where the greenie is lost if the player three putts. In that case, the greenie is awarded to the player second closest the hole.

If one player wins all five points on a hole, points awarded are doubled. Ten points are won.

At the end of the round, the points are totaled and the player with the most points wins.

6 Vegas Shoot-out

Vegas or Daytona as it is known in some parts of the country is a foursome game that can get extremely interesting.

Combined scores are counted for each team. For example, if team A shoots a par 4 and bogey 5, while team B shoots a bogey 5 and triple bogey 7, team A wins 57 minus 45 or **12 points.**

If team A scores a birdie, team B's score is reversed. For example, if team A scores a birdie 4 and a bogey 6 on a par 5 while team B scores a par 5 and a triple bogey 8, team A wins 85 minus 46 points or **39 points.**

Points can be won when you lose a hole! If one member of team A scores 10 or higher on a hole, even though the hole is won by the other member of the team, the score on the hole is reversed.

For example, if team A's score is a par 4 and 10, while team B scores two bogey 5's, team B wins 104 minus 55 or **49 points.**

This game has been known to strain a few friendships!

7 | Wolf

Wolf is a game of strategy played widely throughout the country.

The order of play is decided on the first tee, either by tossing a tee or by the longest drive. *Player one is the wolf on the first hole.* Player two is the wolf on the second, player three on the third, etc. *The wolf rotates on each hole.* Each player is the wolf four times, with the 17th and 18th played in normal rotation or decided by the longest drive.

After everyone has driven, *the wolf picks a partner* for the hole and the *hole is played as a low ball match.* If the hole is tied, no points are scored. If the wolf or his or her partner wins low ball, they win a point.

The wolf has the option of not selecting a partner and playing the hole alone. For example, if all other players hit poor tee shots, OB, into water hazards, etc., *the lone wolf can win three points by going it alone.* If one player ties the wolf, no points are scored. *If the wolf loses the hole to any one player, he or she loses three points, one to each opponent.*

Variations to the Basic Game.

The wolf must choose or pass on a partner immediately after each tee shot. If the second in rotation hits into the rough, the wolf can 'pass' and hope that the third or fourth player hits a half-decent tee shot. If the third hits OB, the wolf is stuck with the fourth as a partner or can go it alone.

A second variation comes into play on par 3's. If a player is wolf, he or she has the option of going for wolf (playing alone) immediately after his or her shot but before anyone else has hit.

If he or she passes, the wolf must pick a partner after all four have hit.

A third variation:

The stakes double on lone-wolf holes. Also the player who is picked can dump the original wolf and go it alone.

This game can be a lot of fun!

8 Six-Point Game

This is an interesting and popular game for threesomes.

Six points are awarded on each hole.

- ***Clear low ball*** is awarded 4 points
- ***Clear second low*** ball earns 2 points
- ***Tie for second low ball*** – 1 point to each player
- ***Two tie for low ball*** – 3 points for each player
- ***All tie for low ball*** – 2 points for each player

9 Defender

This is another popular game for threesomes.

Each player 'defends' three consecutive holes. The order is decided by lot. After all three players have defended, the rotation is then repeated. Each player, therefore, defends a total of six holes.

The 'defender' wins a point each time the defender beats their opponent's score on the hole.

10 On the Perch

The order on the first tee is determined in the usual way.

The player with the honor is 'on the perch' until either the second or third player wins a hole. The winner of the hole is then 'on the perch'.

A point is awarded if the player 'on the perch' beats the better ball of the other two.

Players use handicaps as they appear on the card.

11 Nine

Each hole is worth 9 points.

- ***Outright winner*** earns 5 points
- ***Runner-up*** earns 3 points
- ***Loser*** gets 1 point
- ***Two tie for low ball*** – 4 points each
- ***Two tie for runner-up*** – 2 points each
- ***Three way tie*** – 3 points each

At the end of the round, the points are totaled and the difference calculated.

12 Phantom Pro

Also known as ***'Par for a Partner'.*** Round Robins or Hollywoods can be played with one player having an imaginary partner who shoots par on every hole. On the seventh and thirteenth hole, a new player gets the phantom pro. High handicappers can play a variation of this game where the phantom pro shoots bogey on each hole.

7
8
9
10
11
12

13 Bingo, Bango, Bongo

This is probably the 'granddaddy' of golf's fun games.

Three points are awarded on each hole.

- ***One point (Bingo)*** for the first golfer on the green
- ***One point (Bango)*** for nearest to the pin after all players are on the green
- ***One point (Bongo)*** for the first in the hole or the longest putt sunk

Note: Players are not allowed to putt out to score the Bongo point. Players hit in order, that is, the farthest from the hole hits first.

Variations on this game include a ***doubling of the points awarded*** if one player wins all three points on one hole and a ***tripling of the points awarded*** if all three points are won with a natural birdie.

14 Bong

Bong or Disaster is a game that assesses points against a golfer who makes mistakes on the course. Playing Bong will quickly point out where weaknesses in your game lie. In this game, **the player with the least points wins.**

Situation	Value
Hitting into a bunker	1 point
Hitting into the water	1 point
Leaving a shot in the bunker	2 points
Out-of-bounds	2 points
Lost ball	2 points
Three-putt	3 points
Leaving two shots in a bunker	3 points
Whiffing	4 points
Four-putt	4 points

Playing Bong is a great way to highlight areas of your game that need improvement.

15 Trash

Trash is a series of side games with a million variations.

Listed below are a few of the more common ones. Most get a point. This game can be played with any number of players.

Situation	Value
Hole in one or double eagle	100 points
Eagle	(2 under par on a hole) 50 points
Greenie	Hitting the green in regulation and being closest to the hole. One variation is that a greenie is lost if the player three-putts the hole. The greenie then goes to the second closest player.
Arnie	Making par after hitting the green in regulation without hitting the fairway.
Tiger	Hitting the longest drive on the fairway.
Sandie	Up and down from a bunker.
Birdie	Playing one under par.
Polie	Either sinking a putt longer than the flagstick or hitting an approach shot (in regulation) within the length of the flagstick.
Fish	Making par after hitting into a water hazard.
Chi-Chi	Making par after missing both the fairway and green in regulation.
Hogan	Making par or better after hitting the fairway and green in regulation.
Snakie	Three-putting (minus one point)
Double Snakie	Four-putting (minus two points)

16 Snake

Snake or barracuda is a first rate putting game that adds a tremendous amount of fun to a round of golf.

The first player to three-putt is said to 'hold the snake'. The player passes the snake to the next player who three-putts.

Whoever holds the snake at the ninth or eighteenth loses.

This is the ultimate putting game and can lead to unbelievable pressure putts on the last few holes.

13

14

15

16

Cascades, The Homestead, VA

Side Games

17 Rabbit

There are a number of variations to this popular game.

On the first hole, the rabbit is 'on the loose'. **The first player to win a hole outright is said to 'hold the rabbit'.** If a second player wins a hole outright, the rabbit is 'on the loose' again.

The player who holds the rabbit on the ninth or eighteenth wins.

18 Presses

Presses are side games designed to allow players or teams who are losing a Nassau or similar game to get back into the match.

Usually a team must be two points down in a match before pressing their opponents.

The original game continues but a 'second' match is started with a press.

For example, if a player is two down on the seventh tee and presses the nine, essentially **a new three hole match is started.** If the player wins two of the next three holes, he or she wins the press. Usually a nine hole press is an automatic eighteen hole press as well.

In the above scenario, if player A wins the seventh and eighth hole but loses the ninth, player A wins the press (two holes to one) but loses the original Nassau (four holes to five). If player A wins the seventh and eighth hole and ties the ninth, A wins the press and the original nine is tied.

Usually player B can re-press if he or she finds they are down in the press.

In a normal press, the player who is up in a match has the option of not accepting a press.

Variations to the regular press include automatic presses when one side is one or two points down in a match. Players decide before teeing off what conditions apply to the game.

19 Bisques

Bisques are an interesting variation of handicap strokes. Whereas handicap strokes must be taken on specific holes in a match, bisques can be taken on any hole.

For example, if a 16 handicap player is playing a 10 handicap opponent, the higher handicap player would be given three bisques (half the differential).

The player can declare a bisque before leaving the green, and is limited to one bisque per hole.

Bisques are extremely useful in any game involving carryovers.

Proper Grip

Importance: Nothing is more important to your game than a 'proper' grip. Without this essential element, you are wasting your time and resources trying to refine your game. A poor grip encourages slicing, hooking, and countless other faults that discourage the aspiring golfer.

The basic objective of a proper grip is to unify the hands to work as one cohesive force to align the clubface squarely at impact. A correct grip allows a golfer to consistently swing through the ball at an exact right angle to the intended line of flight.

Left Hand Grip (Firmness)

With the clubhead flat on the ground, (at right angles to the target), grip the club so that the shaft runs diagonally across the palm. Now close the left hand so that the V formed by the thumb and forefinger points to the right shoulder.

The left hand provides firmness in the swing with the shaft held firmly between the butt of the palm and the last two fingers (especially the little finger).

Right Hand Grip (Power)

The right hand grip is primarily a finger grip with the club being held in the 'roots' of the fingers. **The palm should be square to the target** thus encouraging the clubface to be square to the target line at impact.

Place the right hand over the left with the 'lifeline' of the right palm covering the left thumb. The right little finger should overlap the first finger of the left hand. The V formed by the right thumb and forefinger should point between the right shoulder and chin.

Incorrect Grips:

- **Strong Grip:** Encourages a hook and low shot by 'closing' the clubface at impact. Three or four knuckles of the left hand are visible at address.

- **Weak Grip:** Encourages slicing and skied shots by opening the face at impact. No knuckles of the left hand are visible at address.

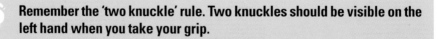 **Remember the 'two knuckle' rule. Two knuckles should be visible on the left hand when you take your grip.**

A proper grip squares the clubface to the target at impact. Shaft should run diagonally across the palm. Last two fingers hold the shaft most firmly.

Grip with the left hand so that the 'V' formed by the thumb and first finger point to the right shoulder.

The 'lifeline' crease of the right hand should cover the left thumb.

Overlap the 'pinkie' of the right hand over the first finger of the left.

A weak grip causes slices and skied shots.

A strong grip encourages hooks and low shots.

V formed by right thumb and forefinger points between the right shoulder and chin.

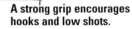

Two knuckles should be visible at address.

Definition: Stance is simply defined as the position of the feet while hitting the ball. Since stance determines the alignment of the hips and shoulders during the swing, a clear understanding of the basic stances can eliminate many 'swing' faults that affect medium and high-handicappers' scores.

Square Stance: As illustrated in the top diagram, both feet are parallel to the line of flight. This aligns the shoulders and hips parallel to the direction the shot will travel. ***A square set-up encourages the golfer to swing the club along the intended line of flight through impact.***

As illustrated opposite, the right foot is more or less at right angles to the target line, thus preventing overswinging. The left foot is 'opened' 30 to 40 degrees to permit an easier hip turn through impact.

For less supple golfers, angle the right foot 5 to 10 degrees away from the target to facilitate a fuller swing.

Open Stance: The left foot is withdrawn from the intended line of flight. While some pros take a slightly open stance with short irons, an open stance when using other clubs (woods, long, and medium irons) will cause the ball to fade or slice. This causes the clubhead to travel from an 'out' to 'in' position across the target line, imparting ***'clockwise'*** sidespin to the ball.

Closed Stance: The right foot is pulled back relative to the left. This produces an 'inside-out' swing, encouraging a hook or draw by imparting ***'counterclockwise' sidespin*** to the ball.

Width of Stance: While this varies from golfer to golfer, the feet should be approximately 'shoulder-width' for good balance.

- Too wide a stance restricts body turn and tends to increase club loft.

- Too narrow a stance encourages spinning out and loss of balance and control.

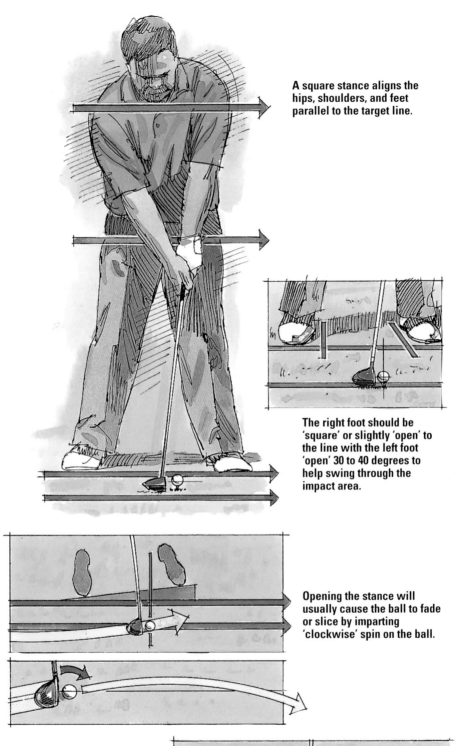

A square stance aligns the hips, shoulders, and feet parallel to the target line.

The right foot should be 'square' or slightly 'open' to the line with the left foot 'open' 30 to 40 degrees to help swing through the impact area.

Opening the stance will usually cause the ball to fade or slice by imparting 'clockwise' spin on the ball.

Closing the stance will cause the ball to draw or hook by putting 'counterclockwise' spin on the ball.

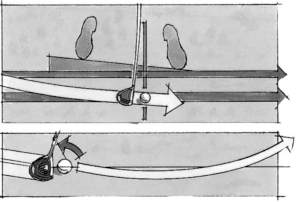

When preparing to stroke the ball, the following 'pro-pointers' should help improve your game and increase consistency.

Club Placement: Before assuming your stance, place the clubhead behind the ball, at right angles to the line of flight. Set the club exactly square to the target. The sole of the club should be flat on the ground. ***The majority of touring pros start their swing sequence by setting the club down before assuming a stance.*** This helps with proper alignment.

Body Position: Position yourself comfortably from the ball, knees slightly flexed, with your left arm fully extended and elbows close together. ***Don't over-reach for the ball.***

Stance: Assume a square or slightly open stance on all full shots. Play the ball just inside your left heel.

Keep Weight Inside: To prevent lateral sway during the swing, try to ***bear your weight 50–50 between your heels and toes.*** Try to keep your body weight to the 'inside' of your stance.

Correct Shoulder Position: Many chronic slicers position their right shoulder too high at address. ***Keep the right shoulder down in relation to the left.*** This facilitates the right shoulder moving under the chin at impact, producing a more vertical swing plane. This swing plane keeps the clubface square to the target through the impact zone.

Keep Hands Close to the Body: Avoid the tendency to over-reach for the ball. The hands should hang comfortably, fairly close to the body to assure a more upright swing plane.

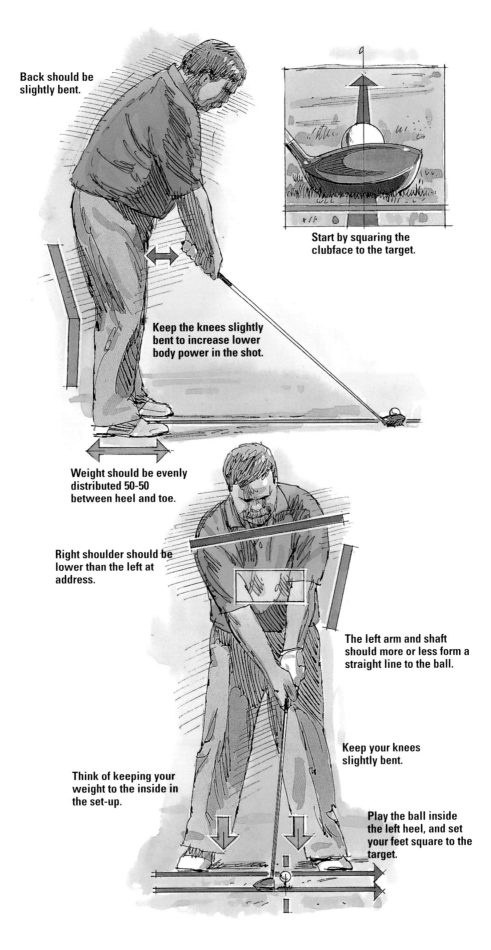

Back should be slightly bent.

Start by squaring the clubface to the target.

Keep the knees slightly bent to increase lower body power in the shot.

Weight should be evenly distributed 50-50 between heel and toe.

Right shoulder should be lower than the left at address.

The left arm and shaft should more or less form a straight line to the ball.

Keep your knees slightly bent.

Think of keeping your weight to the inside in the set-up.

Play the ball inside the left heel, and set your feet square to the target.

The Waggle and Forward Press

The Waggle: The first phase of any good golf swing should be the 'waggle'. This is a series of *loose back and forth movements of the club behind the ball.* Move the clubhead 12 to 24 inches from the ball along the backswing and downswing club path. Set the club down immediately before starting the backswing.

A key swing thought during the waggle is to relax both forearms and shoulders. Stay relaxed during the complete swing. A relaxed upper body is critical for good tempo and increased power off the tee.

This simple step is guaranteed to relax your swing. In addition to eliminating an uncoordinated, jerky start, the direction of the waggle 'path' reinforces that you are aligned properly.

The Forward Press: Most of today's top golfers use a forward press to initiate their swing in a smooth, balanced fashion.

For most, the press is simply a *slight movement of the hands towards the target* that starts the swing motion in an unhurried, coordinated manner.

Others, most notably Gary Player, initiate the press by 'kicking' the right knee towards the target.

Jack Nicklaus uses what he calls a 'stationary press'. This is simply a firming up of the grip immediately before the backswing.

Whatever variation you use, do not forget the press. It eases tension and is sure to eliminate those jerky frozen starts.

4

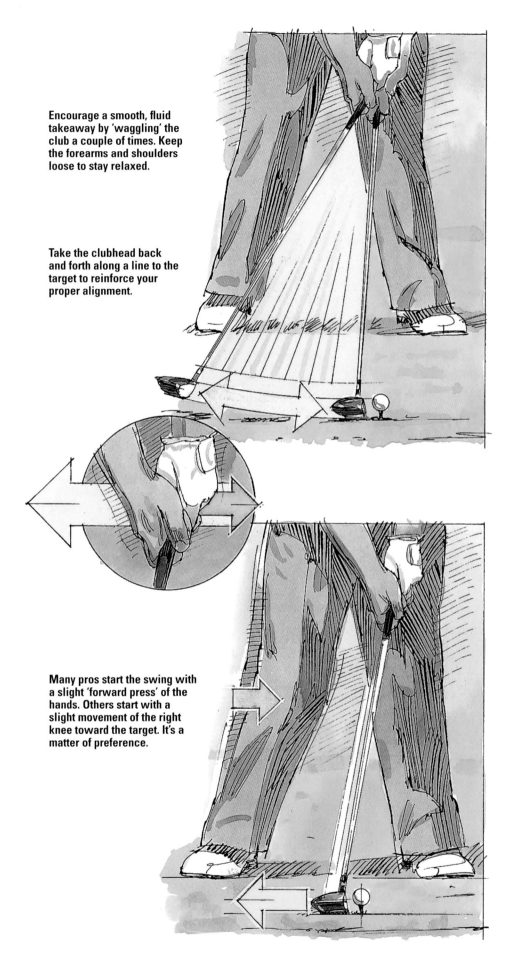

Encourage a smooth, fluid takeaway by 'waggling' the club a couple of times. Keep the forearms and shoulders loose to stay relaxed.

Take the clubhead back and forth along a line to the target to reinforce your proper alignment.

Many pros start the swing with a slight 'forward press' of the hands. Others start with a slight movement of the right knee toward the target. It's a matter of preference.

The Backswing

Although the intricacies of the backswing are best explained by your local pro, here are just a few of the basics that form the foundation of a good consistent golf swing.

Start Low and Slow: This is a *fundamental rule* all golfers should remember. The first 12 to 24 inches of the takeback must be kept deliberately slow. A smooth start is the basis for a more consistent swing.

The 'low' takeback guarantees good extension, a wide backswing arc, and a proper 'coiled' shoulder position at the top.

Straight Left Arm: For more power and consistency, *keep the left arm and club in a straight line until well into the backswing.* The wrists will then 'cock' naturally. In other words, the right hand should not be used to pull the clubhead back. Push the right hand away from the ball.

Vertical Swing Plane for Accuracy: The more vertical a swing plane, the more accurate your game will be. The bottom diagram illustrates an ideal swing plane. Note how my left arm points down towards the ball at the top of the backswing. Any flat 'baseball' swing invites problems. Notice how *my left shoulder tucks under the right at the top.*

The Right Elbow Tuck: The 'Flying Elbow' is a common problem. Think of pointing the right elbow downwards throughout the swing.

Avoid Swaying: Probably the most common expression in golf is to keep the head down. The basis for consistent play is to keep the head relatively steady with the swing naturally rotating around the head. Any excessive head sway will cause all sorts of mishits.

Keep the left arm and shaft in a straight line at the start of the backswing.

Keep your head relatively steady throughout the swing. Point your chin at the ball and coil around your head.

Start back 'low and slow'. Keeping it low for the first 24 inches widens the swing arc and increases power and distance.

Clubhead should point to the target at the top of the backswing.

Avoid the 'flying' elbow and try to keep your right elbow pointing downwards. This will help take the club back inside.

Swing on a more or less vertical swing plane for greater accuracy. A flat 'horizontal' swing will produce slices and pulls.

Downswing and Follow-through

To initiate a smooth rhythmical swing, try pausing slightly at the top of your backswing. This lessens any chance of a jerky, uncoordinated downswing.Practice the following 'pro-pointers' for greater distance and accuracy.

Keep Relaxed: Mentally try to ***keep the forearms and shoulders relaxed*** at the beginning of the downswing. The tendency of a great number of high handicappers is to tighten up at the top and lunge at the ball.

Start with the Hips and Legs: The proper downswing starts with the lower body. The right foot begins the downswing by pushing towards the target causing the knees to move laterally in the direction the shot is to be played. The hips slide towards the target therefore pulling the left shoulder and arm into the ball.

Avoid Head Sway: Stay behind the ball. Some high handicappers move their heads laterally towards the target during the downswing. ***The head should remain relatively steady and well back of the ball until after impact.*** Any forward sway actually decreases clubhead speed at impact.

Right Shoulder under the Left: Passing the ***right shoulder under the left*** assures an upright vertical swing plane. This keeps the clubface on the right track through the impact area. Failure of the right shoulder to pass under the left can result in an all too common 'baseball' swing and resultant slice.

Swing through the Ball to Target: Many golfers unconsciously let up on their swing at impact. Complete your swing with ***good extension towards the target.*** Finish high with a firm grip. Any loosening of the grip at impact will result in loss of distance.

If you are spinning out of the shot, your swing plane is too flat. Study professional golfers on tour and try to mimic their finishes. A good finish will knock strokes off your handicap.

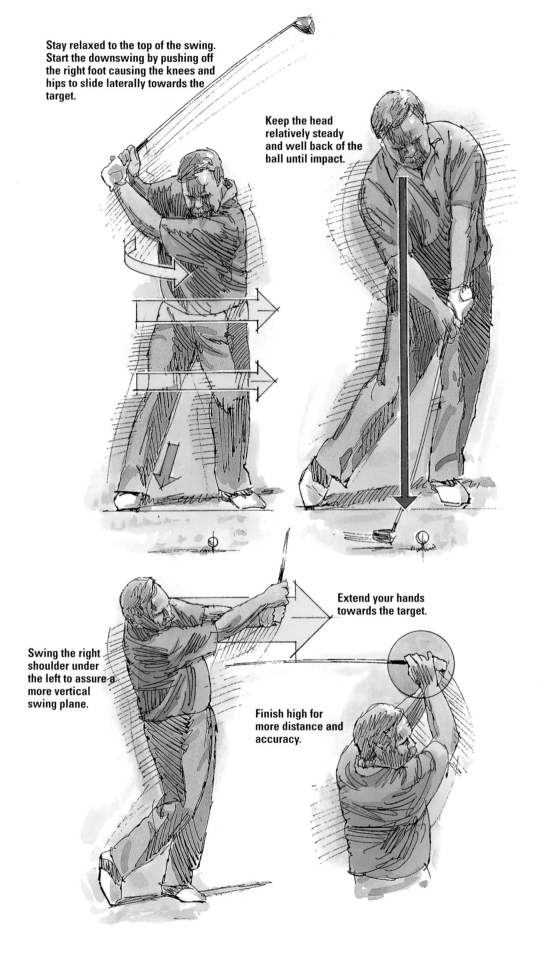

Stay relaxed to the top of the swing. Start the downswing by pushing off the right foot causing the knees and hips to slide laterally towards the target.

Keep the head relatively steady and well back of the ball until impact.

Swing the right shoulder under the left to assure a more vertical swing plane.

Extend your hands towards the target.

Finish high for more distance and accuracy.

Playing 'smarter' on a golf course is something all of us could benefit from. Improved course management can make a big difference in your game, so try to incorporate these changes into every round of golf.

Aim Away from Trouble: If you have extreme trouble on the left of the hole, tee to the left and drive away from that point. This 'opens' the hole, giving you a larger target to hit to.

Think positively. If you have to carry water, don't let negative thoughts dominate your swing. Think of a positive swing thought when setting up and concentrate on nailing your shot to the target.

Think Target not Distance: Many weekend golfers (as well as a few of the pros on tour) want to 'rip' drivers on every hole. There are several situations where going to a 3 wood or long iron is the smart thing to do.

On short par 4's, a long drive may leave you with a difficult 50 or 60 yard half-wedge. Playing a 3 or 5 wood off the tee will allow you to approach the green with an easier full wedge or 9 iron. The same applies to approaches to short par 5's. Trying to hit a hard 3 wood into a tight green will most likely leave you in a green-side bunker. ***Play your second to a target that will allow you to hit a full short iron into the green.***

If a good drive will leave you with a severe downhill or uphill lie, or the hole funnels into a tight landing area, leave the driver in the bag. Avoid trouble by playing to a flat landing area or short of the narrow fairway.

On many short, dogleg par 4's and 5's, course designers love to guard the inside corner with a bunker. Play short. Many of these holes can be reached easily without hitting the driver.

Play for easier approaches to the green: Always try to drive to a safe landing area that will allow for the easiest approach to the green. This target may change depending on the pin placement.

Playing to Tight Pins: It's usually best for mid to high handicappers to avoid going for a pin located tight to a green-side hazard. Play more to the center of the green, take your two putts and get to the next hole.

Playing to Severely Sloped Greens: Play your approach so that you give yourself the opportunity to putt uphill.

Match Play: If your opponent has hit into a hazard or OB, play conservatively. Why risk a difficult shot when a bogey will probably win the hole?

If you are faced with a 'delicate' lob to a tight pin, play more to the center of the green and play for two putts.

On the green, if a two putt has a good chance of winning the hole, play a putt that 'dies' at the pin. Getting aggressive here will probably leave you a difficult 4 or 5 footer coming back.

Water left. Tee left and hit away from trouble.

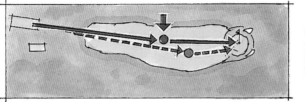

On short par 4's, play for a full approach shot to the green.

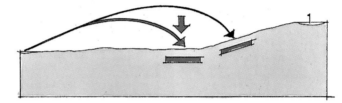

Avoid severely sloped or narrow landing areas.

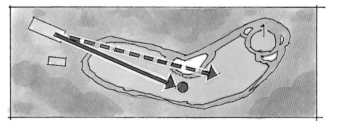

On short dog-legs, play a 3 wood versus a driver to avoid fairway bunkers.

Avoid going for 'sucker' pins. Play to the center of the green.

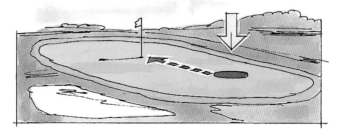

Play for uphill putts on severely sloped greens.

Nothing is more satisfying in golf than consistently hitting long drives down the center of the fairway.

Once you have mastered the swing basics in the previous sections, use the following 'pro-pointers' to checklist your swing.

Stance	Square
Grip	Remember the 'two knuckle' rule
	Left hand 'V' to the right shoulder
Ball Position	Opposite the left heel
Shoulder Position	Not directly pointing to the target but parallel to it
Weight	Keep it centered and inside
Waggle	Assures a smooth swing
Backswing	Low and slow
	Vertical swing plane for accuracy
Downswing	Avoid head sway
	Swing through the ball to target
	Finish high

Swing Tip: Developing a smooth and rhythmical swing can do more for your drives than any attempt to 'power' the shot. **Don't try to kill the ball.** The vast majority of touring pros swing at 70 to 80 percent of their capacity unless an extra 20 to 30 yards is an absolute necessity.

Teeing Tip: Tee up the ball so that one half of it is above the top of the driver. When using irons on par 3's, always tee up the ball to assure a consistent lie.

Drive Away from Trouble: When playing near an out-of-bounds area, tee the ball nearest the OB area and drive away from it. You will approach the fairway from the greatest angle and hit away from trouble.

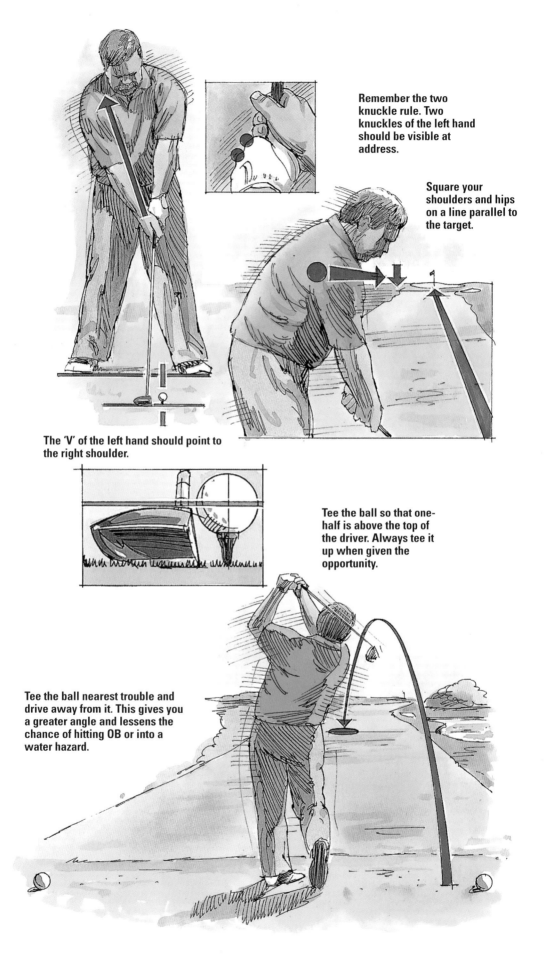

Remember the two knuckle rule. Two knuckles of the left hand should be visible at address.

Square your shoulders and hips on a line parallel to the target.

The 'V' of the left hand should point to the right shoulder.

Tee the ball so that one-half is above the top of the driver. Always tee it up when given the opportunity.

Tee the ball nearest trouble and drive away from it. This gives you a greater angle and lessens the chance of hitting OB or into a water hazard.

Grip it right! One of first things to check when trying for more distance is your grip. The best grip for maximum distance is a 'fingers' grip rather than a 'palms' or 'fisty' grip. Many short hitters grab the club like a baseball bat, in the palms rather than in the fingers. A 'fingers' grip allows the club to release through the impact zone.

Grip it light! Short hitters grip the club too hard when trying to rip a drive for maximum distance. A 'death grip' on the club increases tightness in the forearms and shoulders, causing a stiff, tense take-away. Grip it light and stay loose!

Swing thought: Sam Snead once said that you should grip the club as lightly as if you are holding a small bird in your hand. It's a good analogy. The next time you want to out-drive your buddies, think of Slammin' Sammy's bird!

Power flex the knees! Many short hitters use only the upper body to power their shots. They take lower body strength out of the swing by standing straight-legged in the setup. Typically the short hitter starts the downswing with a shoulder turn instead of a lateral hip slide toward the target. A common result is a weak slice since the lower body does not 'clear' before the shoulders and arms.

Flex your knees in the setup. Start your downswing with the lower body by pushing off the right foot, driving the lower body towards the target. Your lower body now leads rather than follows the downswing.

Swing it back slow! The majority of touring pros think of a slow, smooth backswing as a primary swing thought when trying for more distance! Jack Nicklaus has always described it as being more deliberate in the set-up and takeaway.

Contrast that with the swings of many amateurs. The most common tendency is to swing fast and rip at the ball.

Set up the power drive with a slow, tension-free backswing. Make a smooth unhurried transition at the top. Then gradually accelerate through impact to a high finish.

Widen your swing arc! Many amateurs narrow the swing 'radius' by picking up the club early in the backswing. The wrists 'break' early in the swing, robbing the shot of power and distance.

Keep the club head close to the ground for the first 18 to 24 inches. Extend the club and left arm low to the ground at the start of the backswing, with the right elbow gradually folding or tucking to your right side.

A bit of advice. Don't force this move to the point of swaying off the ball and losing your balance. Stay loose and swing back 'low and slow'.

Use a 'fingers' grip to help release the club through impact.

Keep a light grip for maximum distance.

Flex the knees for maximum distance. This adds lower-body power to the shot.

Start the downswing by pushing off the right foot.

Keep a slow, smooth backswing as your primary swing thought when going for distance. Widen your swing arc by keeping the club-head close to the ground for the first 18 to 24 inches. Swing back low and slow!

SLOW

Power coil: The more 'coil' you put in your drives, the more distance you're going to get with your driver.

Increase clubhead speed by increasing your upper body turn. Think of turning your back to the target at the top of the backswing. The hip turn should only be one-half that of the shoulders. This creates tension or 'winds the spring' between the upper and lower body.

On the downswing, stay loose with the shoulders and arms to prevent the urge to lunge at the ball. Turn your hips early in the swing and finish with your belt buckle facing the target area.

Swing thought: Remember that the power of the drive comes from coiling on the takeback and uncoiling on the downswing. The arms produce little of the power. Keep the hands and shoulders 'loose' and let the uncoiling torso whip the club through the impact zone.

Extend to a high finish! A full finish will add yards to your drives. A common tendency when trying for greater distance is to swing harder. Many slicers come 'over the top' or 'cast' the club. This leads to an even greater 'out to in' swing path causing an even worse slice. Power is lost by hitting across the ball with the clubface open.

Harness the power of the swing by two simple swing adjustments.

First, take back the club with a straight left arm. Tuck your right elbow close to the body. This creates an 'inside to outside' swing path.

Second, extend through the target to a high, balanced finish. This releases the clubhead through impact.

Swing thought: Try to copy the high finish you see with the guys on tour. Don't worry about ripping the ball. The high finish will get you an extra 10 to 15 yards off the tee.

Draw the ball for distance! If you chronically slice the ball, consider adjusting your setup to encourage a draw.

The draw's swing path is 'in to out' and imparts 'counterclockwise' sidespin to the ball. The ball lands 'hotter' and rolls farther than a slice or fade.

Take a 'stronger' grip than usual. Stronger means hand position not grip strength. Rotate your left hand so that three knuckles are visible at address. This helps close the clubface at impact.

Close your stance. Drop your right foot back a couple of inches. This aims your hips and shoulders slightly right of the target. A closed stance helps an 'in to out' swing path.

Try this on the range. Find the least adjustment that will straighten your slice. You can gain 20 to 30 yards by incorporating these setup changes.

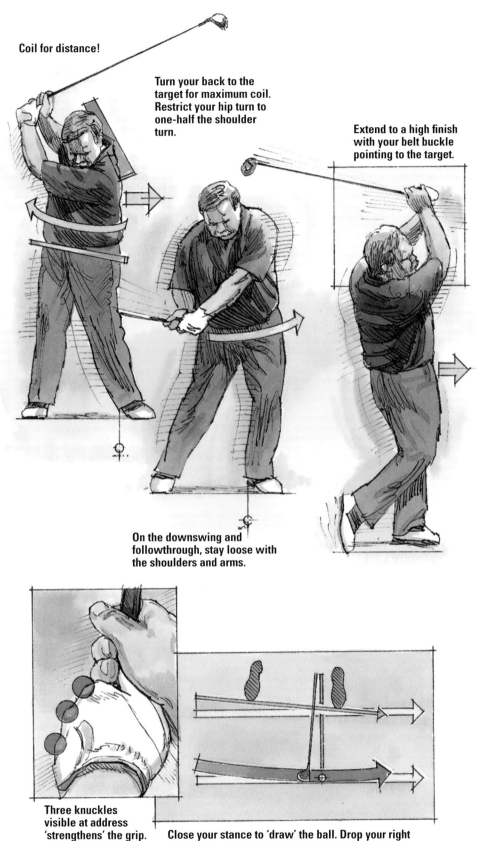

Coil for distance!

Turn your back to the target for maximum coil. Restrict your hip turn to one-half the shoulder turn.

Extend to a high finish with your belt buckle pointing to the target.

On the downswing and followthrough, stay loose with the shoulders and arms.

Three knuckles visible at address 'strengthens' the grip.

Close your stance to 'draw' the ball. Drop your right foot back a couple of inches. This creates an 'in to out' swing path, and puts 'counterclockwise' overspin on the ball.

Try a longer shaft. Traditional steel-shafted drivers commonly use a 43 inch shaft. Many of the newer graphite-shafted drivers increase the length to 44 or 45 inches. The longer shaft lengthens the swing arc and increases clubhead speed at impact. The downside to a longer shaft is that the club is harder to control. If you tend to spray your drives, this may not be for you.

Stads cheap tip. If you are comfortable and consistent with your current driver, try this. When its time to regrip, have the shop add a one or two inch 'plug' to the shaft. It's an inexpensive option to try, and allows you to stick with the driver you are comfortable with.

Check your flex. The right flex in your club shaft adds extra distance to your drives. As you make your transition at the top, the shaft 'loads' or bends. Accelerating on the downswing, the shaft bends further until just before impact. Entering the impact zone, the shaft straightens and 'kicks' into the ball adding what is termed 'kick velocity' at impact. This can add 10 mph to the initial velocity of the ball.

Shafts come in a number of flexes. Equipment manufacturers now complement regular, stiff, and extra stiff flex shafts with a range of intermediate options. Follow the guidelines listed below.

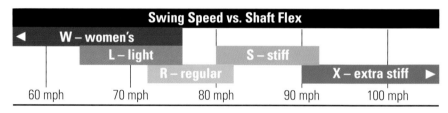

Ask a golf professional to help determine what flex best suits your game.

Stad's quick tip. If you usually hook the ball, a stiffer shaft (less flex) may straighten your drives. If you slice or hit to the right, a more flexible shaft will give more 'kick' at impact and help close the clubface.

Try the new technology. If you are still using traditional woods and want greater distance, new metal woods are the way to go.

It's not just advertising hype. Golf manufacturers have made tremendous strides in club design over the last few years. The new oversize metal drivers are more forgiving on mis-hit shots. It's simple physics. Metal heads are usually foam filled shells. More weight is distributed to the perimeter of the clubface. This increases the sweetspot and adds distance on mishits.

Will titanium help? There's good reason why manufacturers are going to the new titanium technology. Titanium is stronger than the traditional steel used in driver heads. It's also 40 percent lighter. This allows the club designer to increase the size of the head without increasing the weight. The equipment gurus can engineer more weight into the perimeter of the clubhead, thus giving an even larger sweetspot.

Titanium is more expensive than traditional steel or wood. If you are considering a new set of clubs, make the investment. You should be able to drive the ball farther with fewer mis-hits.

(continued on following pages ▶)

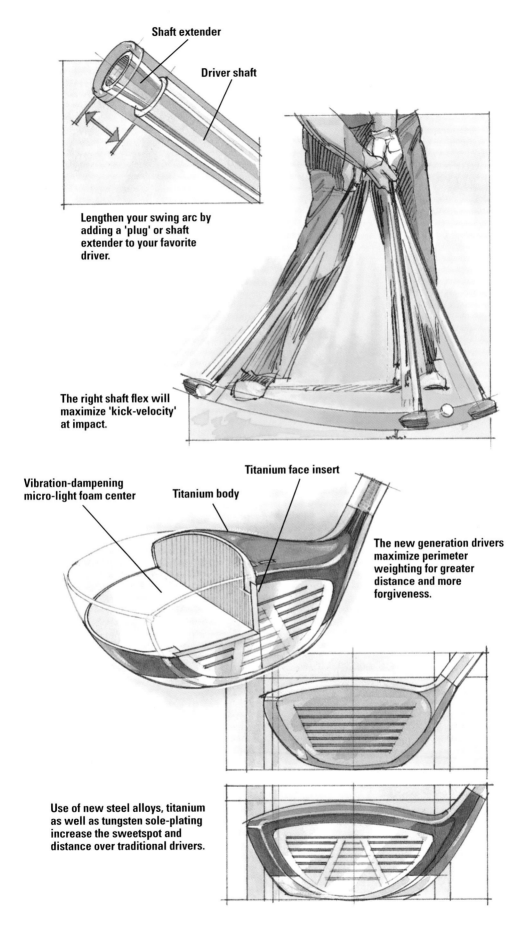

Shaft extender

Driver shaft

Lengthen your swing arc by adding a 'plug' or shaft extender to your favorite driver.

The right shaft flex will maximize 'kick-velocity' at impact.

Titanium face insert

Vibration-dampening micro-light foam center

Titanium body

The new generation drivers maximize perimeter weighting for greater distance and more forgiveness.

Use of new steel alloys, titanium as well as tungsten sole-plating increase the sweetspot and distance over traditional drivers.

(continued from the preceding pages ◀)

Find the right loft for your swing. One of the most important things for maximum distance is to find the right loft for your driver. Driver lofts usually vary from 7 to 12 degrees for touring professionals.

Low handicappers who generate a lot of clubhead speed (90 plus mph) need less loft to launch the ball on an ideal trajectory. Average players need 10 to 11 degrees. If you don't generate a lot of clubhead speed, go to a 12 or 13 degree driver to get the ball airborne for maximum carry and roll.

Equipment tip. Club manufacturers often have demo days at local courses. Check around for schedules. This is probably the easiest way to check out various loft options.

Pick the ball type best suited to your game. If you want to 'fine tune' your game for maximum distance, choosing the right ball is critical. However, if you are like most golfers, it's easy to get confused when trying to differentiate various ball types at your local retailer or pro-shop.

If distance is your primary concern, then stick with '2-piece' balls such as the **Nike Distance ball**. It is designed specifically for maximum distance and durability. If you want greater spin control, try the **Nike Spin Control ball**. It feels more like a tour-level ball because its softer ionomer cover maximizes feel and spin. If you are a little 'wild' off the tee, the **Nike Distance Control ball** is designed to reduce driver sidespin that should help you hit straighter drives.

11

Until recently, there was a trade off between maximum distance and maximum spin control. The new 'dual-cover' balls such as the Nike Tour Accuracy ball are manufactured with a maximum compression core for greater distance, but also have a soft inner-cover called a 'transition' layer. On full irons or wood shots, the inner cover transfers maximum energy to the oversized compression core. This maintains maximum distance.

However, with shorter irons, the soft inner-cover works with the soft urethane outer cover for maximum feel and high spin around the greens.

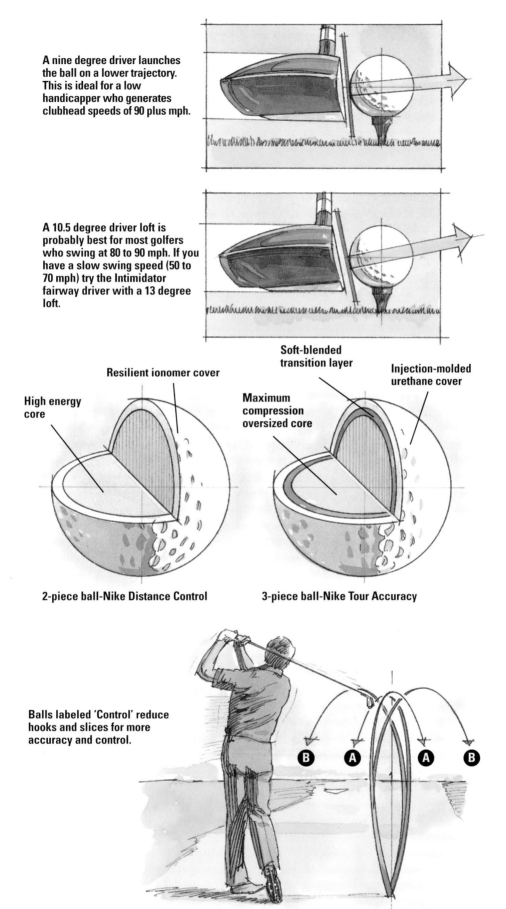

A nine degree driver launches the ball on a lower trajectory. This is ideal for a low handicapper who generates clubhead speeds of 90 plus mph.

A 10.5 degree driver loft is probably best for most golfers who swing at 80 to 90 mph. If you have a slow swing speed (50 to 70 mph) try the Intimidator fairway driver with a 13 degree loft.

High energy core

Resilient ionomer cover

Soft-blended transition layer

Injection-molded urethane cover

Maximum compression oversized core

2-piece ball-Nike Distance Control

3-piece ball-Nike Tour Accuracy

Balls labeled 'Control' reduce hooks and slices for more accuracy and control.

B A A B

A = Nike Distance Control Ball, B = Traditional Ball

The 'donut' drill. Invest a few bucks in a special weight called the donut. They can be found in most pro-shops or golf retailers. On the practice tee, swing the donut 20 or 30 times before hitting a bucket. The added weight will strengthen and stretch the back muscles as well as increase your swing arc. The 'donut' also helps you swing 'through' the ball. Now try the driver alone and watch the ball fly!

The 'stretch' drill. Before practice, make this stretch exercise part of your routine. Place the driver on the back of your neck and grab the club head and grip with your hands. Take a stance and pivot around the top of your spine on a plane similar to a real swing. Try to turn your back to the target. Don't force this exercise! Slowly repeat 20 to 30 times, stretching a little more with each repetition. Try to restrict your hip turn to build more coil into the routine.

The 'extension' drill. On the practice range, tee the ball 6 to 10 inches ahead of your left foot. Try to extend to the ball through your normal extension zone. This will help if you are what is termed 'ball conscious'. Golfers who hit it short tend to stop at the ball at impact.

The 'swing-arc' drill. Place a tee 24 inches behind your teed ball, on an imaginary line to your swing target. Reinforce a low, wide backswing by touching the second tee with your driver's clubhead on the takeback.

The 'two tee' drill. Place a second tee 6 inches ahead of your teed ball. Try to consistently hit the second tee on your follow through. Increase the distance to 12 inches once you've mastered the shorter distance. This drill helps you 'swing through the ball' versus 'hitting at the ball'.

The 'release' drill. If your divots curve to the left and show an open clubface at impact (see diagram) try this drill. On the range, try to square up the clubface by rotating your forearms through the impact zone. Think of turning to touch the forearms on the follow through. A good mental image is to turn your right hand into a 'handshake' position when the club is through the impact zone.

The 'knee flex' drill. It's not the easiest thing in the world to change a set-up you have used for a number of years. The next time you go to a practice range, try this drill. To reinforce just how important the power flex is, try hitting a few balls with an exaggerated 'stiff leg' swing set-up. Swing as hard as you can and note how far your ball carries. Now, flex the knees and hit a few. You are sure to gain 20 to 30 yards on your drives. Remember, this applies to irons as well. Expect more consistency and distance with every club in your bag.

Build coil into your pre-game routine. Try this 20 to 30 times before play.

Use a swing weight or 'donut' to increase your swing arc.

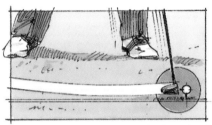

Extension drill: Tee ball 6 to 10 inches ahead of left foot.

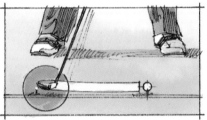

Swing-arc drill: On the backswing, hit the second tee 24 inches behind ball.

Two-tee drill: Hit the second tee on the followthrough.

Divot shows 'open' clubface at impact.

Rotate your arms to increase distance and square the clubface at impact. Turn and touch your forearms through the impact zone.

'Stiff leg' it for weak shots. Power flex to increase your distance!

Fairway Woods (The Game Savers)

Fairway woods are often described as 'game savers'. On long par 4's, these useful clubs allow the average golfer to 'get home' in two shots with an excellent chance at par or birdie.

A basic 'long club' swing is used with only the position of the ball being slightly different.

Stance: I prefer a slightly open stance when hitting fairway woods.

Ball Position: Play the ball one to two inches inside the left heel. This allows the club to strike the ball on the bottom of the swing arc as opposed to the 'teed' ball which is struck a slightly ascending blow.

Swing Basics: If you have a good lie on the fairway, it's best to sweep the ball off the turf. Take a normal 'long club' swing with the clubhead striking the ball before the turf. ***Don't try to force this shot.*** An easy sweeping type of swing is all that is needed. Try emphasizing a low take-back of the club to keep the clubhead low throughout the impact area.

If you have a ***less than ideal lie*** (light rough), play the ball more to the center of your stance and ***play more of a punch shot, hitting down into the ball.*** From an open stance, this shot will fade somewhat, so allow for it when aligning to the target.

Woods	Men's Average Distance (yds)	Women's Average Distance (yds)	Your Average Distance (yds)
Driver	210 and up	180 and up	
Two	200-220	175-185	
Three	190-210	170-180	
Four	180-200	160-170	
Five	170-190	150-160	
Seven	160-180	140-150	

Many golfers are not comfortable hitting fairway woods. The most common swing fault is trying to 'scoop' underneath the ball in order to produce a high trajectory. The tendency for many high handicappers is to lean back at impact with little or no weight transfer. This promotes all sorts of trouble, 'topping' being the most common problem.

Let the loft of the club do the work. Hit slightly downwards into the ball. The built-in loft of the wood will do the rest.

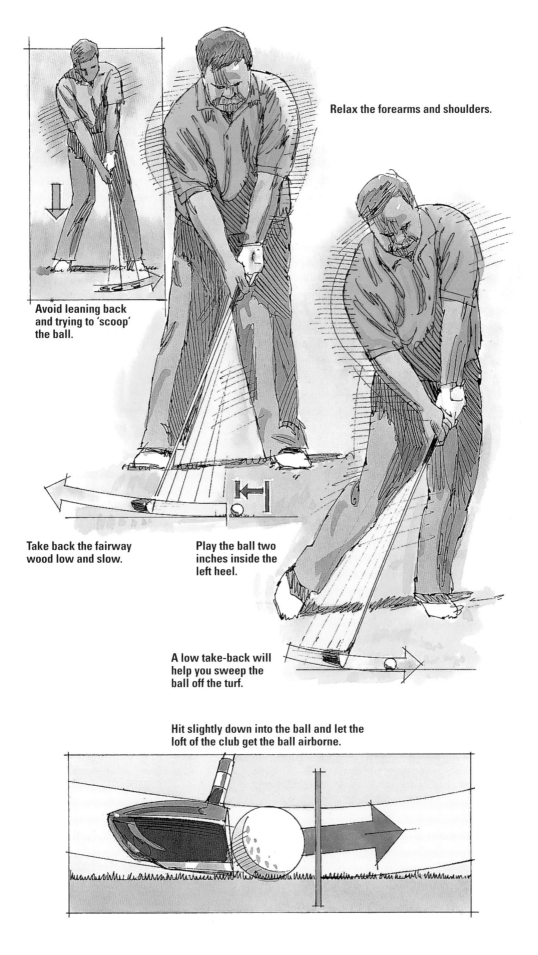

Relax the forearms and shoulders.

Avoid leaning back
and trying to 'scoop'
the ball.

Take back the fairway
wood low and slow.

Play the ball two
inches inside the
left heel.

A low take-back will
help you sweep the
ball off the turf.

Hit slightly down into the ball and let the
loft of the club get the ball airborne.

If you are like most golfers, the long irons are probably the most difficult clubs in your bag to hit consistently. Most mid to high handicappers find it hard to get sufficient loft with the 2 or 3 irons. You have two options here. Avoid the long iron in favor of fairway woods or get to the practice range and work on this part of your game.

Probably the greatest problem for most amateurs is that they 'psyche' themselves out of hitting good long-iron approaches. Tension overcomes the swing and a poor shot results.

Here's how you can improve your long iron play.

Try to swing the long iron like your driver, 3, or 5 wood. Like the fairway woods, ***the long iron shot is basically somewhat of a 'sweeping' motion.*** When setting up for the long iron, think of your basic driver swing with the club striking the ball before the turf.

Stance: Open

Ball Position: I prefer to position the ball farther forward in my stance when hitting the long irons. To aid in hitting down on the ball, the hands should be slightly ahead of the clubhead at address and impact.

Weight Transfer: In order to hit 'crisp' irons, your weight should transfer to the left early in the downswing. Start your downstroke with an early forward hip thrust. This shifts the lowest part of the swing arc ahead of the ball.

Smoothness and Rhythm: Many amateur golfers try too hard with the long irons. ***Don't try to overpower the ball.*** Stay well within your swing and stick to good fundamentals such as the waggle and forward press. Most importantly, ***start the clubhead away from the ball slowly and deliberately.***

Try to approach the long iron with the same mental attitude as a 6 or 7 iron shot. ***Swing well within your limit, concentrating on rhythm rather than power.***

Trouble Shots: The 3 iron is a great club for getting out of trouble situations. If you are 20 to 30 yards into trees and have to keep the shot low, the long iron is your club of choice. Choke down on the club, play the ball back in your stance and swing down into the ball, keeping the hands ahead of the club throughout the swing. Practice this on the range. It's an easy shot to master.

14

If you are uncomfortable over a 2 or 3 iron, think of trying to eliminate muscle tightness in the forearms and shoulders as your primary swing thought.

Practice the long irons before trying to use them on the course. Take one club to the range and devote a few practice sessions to the 3 or 4 iron.

If you are still uncomfortable after giving them a good try, leave the long irons in you trunk and stick with the fairway woods instead. A poorly hit 3 or 5 wood will go a lot further than a mediocre long iron.

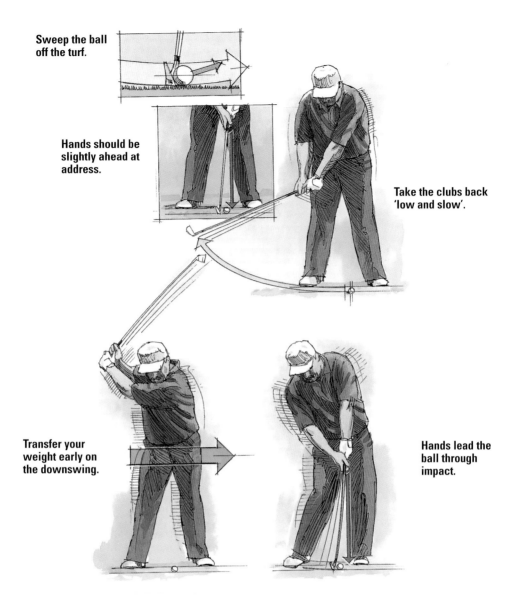

Sweep the ball off the turf.

Hands should be slightly ahead at address.

Take the clubs back 'low and slow'.

Transfer your weight early on the downswing.

Hands lead the ball through impact.

Use a long iron to 'punch' your way out of trouble.

With short to mid irons your primary goal is accuracy.

The built-in loft of the shorter irons makes these clubs easier to use for the average golfer. Since accuracy here is more important than distance, ***don't try to hit the ball with a great deal of force.*** An easy, smooth swing following swing basics outlined in previous sections will deliver accuracy and consistency.

Stance: Use a ***slightly open*** stance with the short to mid irons. This turns the golfer slightly towards the hole and reduces body turn. Depending on the distance from the green, open your stance so that your feet are aligned 15 to 40 feet left of the target. Some teaching professionals recommend that the width of your stance decrease slightly as the loft of your club increases.

Ball Position: As a rule, play the ball a couple of inches inside your left heel. Since the feet are closer together, the ball is played more to the center of the stance.

Address: Stand ***slightly closer*** to the ball to accommodate the shorter shaft length. To check your correct position, the bottom of the clubhead should be flat on the ground, centered behind the golf ball.

Swing Basics: Since accuracy is the key to short iron play, I recommend that you develop a ***more upright swing action*** with these clubs. The more upright the swing plane, the longer the clubhead will travel along the target line through the impact zone. As well, a steeper swing plane will allow you ***to hit down on the ball rather than sweep it.*** A properly hit short iron will take a sizable divot after impact and impart a lot of backspin on the ball. You should be able to 'nail' your short irons close to the hole for more one-putt greens.

Both short and mid iron shots are more compact than a driver or long iron swing. With the narrower stance, the lower body is 'quieter' in the swing, and the hips should rotate less than a drive. On the backswing, consciously swing your arms toward the sky, more upward than around the body. Make sure the hands lead the clubhead at impact.

As with the long irons, ***shift your weight to the left early in the swing and make sure you hit down into the ball.*** Don't worry about getting the ball in the air. The natural loft of the club will accomplish this for you.

15

The greatest fault golfers have in hitting good short irons is trying to swing too hard. Trying to 'rip' a wedge or 9 iron will cause all sorts of swing faults to creep into your swing. Stay well within your capabilities. Use one more club if you need extra distance.

Sometimes golfers let up too early on the more compact 'three-quarter' swing. Remember, don't stop the swing at the ball. Follow through with good extension making sure that the swing pivots around the head. Don't force the short or mid irons.

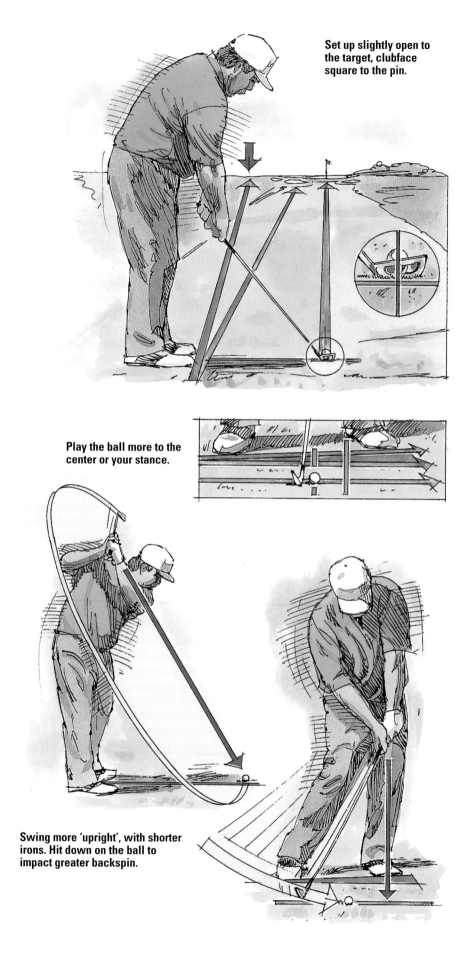

Set up slightly open to the target, clubface square to the pin.

Play the ball more to the center or your stance.

Swing more 'upright', with shorter irons. Hit down on the ball to impact greater backspin.

The Chip

Description: The chip is a ***low trajectory shot*** with a minimum of backspin. Use the least-lofted club to deliver the ball to the green. Follow the swing basics listed below to increase your one-putt greens.

Stance: Assume a slightly open stance with your feet close together.

Ball Position: Play the chip with the ball in the center of your stance, although some teaching pros play it opposite the left heel.

Clubface Alignment: The clubface should be square to the target line to assure accuracy. Read the green as you would a putt and adjust your alignment accordingly.

The Swing: Choke down on your club for greater control. ***Keep your weight on the left side.*** Stroke the ball with a short, crisp swing. ***The hands lead the downstroke,*** allowing the clubface to strike down and through the ball.

Accelerate the club through the ball with little or no wrist motion. Limit your follow-through to the length of the backswing. The ball should 'click' off the club with a low trajectory and run approximately two-thirds of the way to the pin.

Strategy: Chipping near the green with a 7 or 8 iron is a higher percentage shot than pitching with a wedge. ***The chip is more predictable and behaves like a putt.*** A low trajectory shot will run truer than a high-lofted wedge or 9 iron. Also, if you miscue with a wedge, the ball can either be 'knifed' across the green or 'scuffed' an embarrassing foot or two.

Club Selection: Use the ***least-lofted*** club to get you on the green. Most low handicappers use any club from a 5 to 8 iron, with the most popular being the 7 or 8 iron. (See club suggestions in the top diagram).

Planning the Shot: Always chip to a target. ***Pick a spot on the green*** where you want the ball to land and strive to hit the target.

In practice situations, place an object on the green such as a score card or handkerchief and try to consistently drop the ball onto that precise point. Practicing the short game will lower your score much more quickly than spending hours on the range hitting drivers and full iron shots.

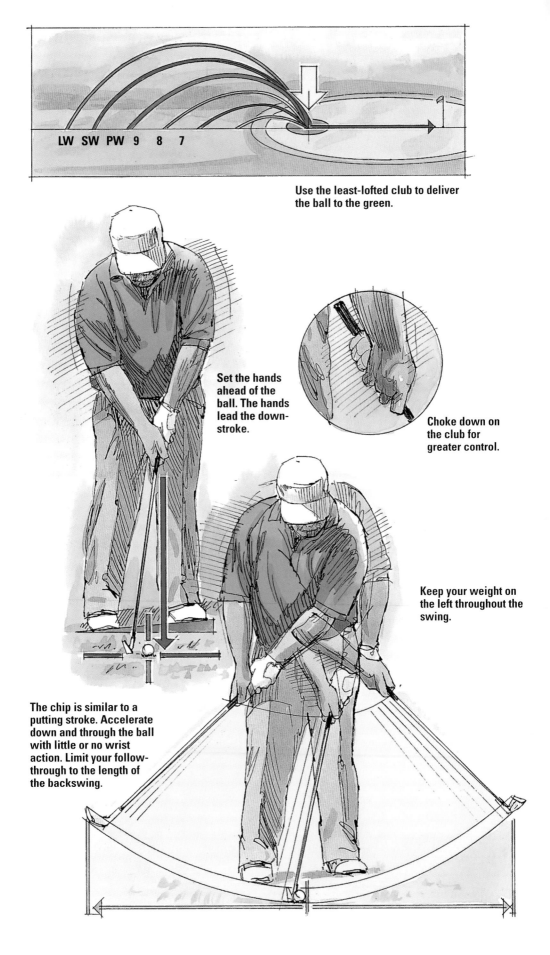

LW SW PW 9 8 7

Use the least-lofted club to deliver the ball to the green.

Set the hands ahead of the ball. The hands lead the downstroke.

Choke down on the club for greater control.

Keep your weight on the left throughout the swing.

The chip is similar to a putting stroke. Accelerate down and through the ball with little or no wrist action. Limit your follow-through to the length of the backswing.

The pitch is a **high trajectory shot** hit with the higher-lofted short irons (8,9, pitching wedge). This shot is best used when the ball is beyond 20 to 25 yards of the green or when obstacles such as bunkers or water hazards must be cleared.

Types of Pitches:

Lofted Pitch: (sand wedge or pitching wedge)

Use this high trajectory shot in the following situations.

- To clear a trap or other hazard with little green to work with.
- To stop the ball on a 'hard' green.
- To hold a green sloped away from you.
- To hold a green when the wind is behind you.

Low Running Pitch: (7, 8, or 9 iron)

Use this less-lofted shot in the following situations.

- When the opening to the green is wide with no intervening obstacles.
- When the green is sloped towards you.
- When hitting into the wind.

Stance: Assume an **open stance** (feet close together) with the left foot drawn back a few inches. This effectively restricts your body action and prevents overswinging.

Ball Position: Ball should be **inside the left heel.** This will vary from golfer to golfer. As a rule, playing the ball forward in your stance will impart greater loft to the shot.

Address: Most of your **weight should be on your left foot at address** and should remain on the left side throughout the swing. **Never shift your weight.** Set your hands ahead of the ball to assure a descending blow into the ball prior to the bottom of the downswing arc.

Swing Basics: Consistent pitch shots call for a **minimum of body movement.** The basic full shot is primarily an 'arms and hands' swing with minimal hip turn. **Limit yourself to a three-quarter backswing,** keeping the left arm straight and allowing your wrists to cock early in the backswing.

17

On the downswing, **hit down and through the ball.** Do not try to scoop under the ball. The high loft of the club will get the ball into the air.

Extend your arms through the impact area, taking a divot after striking the ball.

On low running pitches with 7, 8, or 9 irons, it's critical to keep your weight on the left side. Never shift your weight.

PITCHING POINTER: Swing easily yet firmly. The full wedge and 9 iron are two clubs that cannot be forced. If you need extra distance select a less-lofted club.

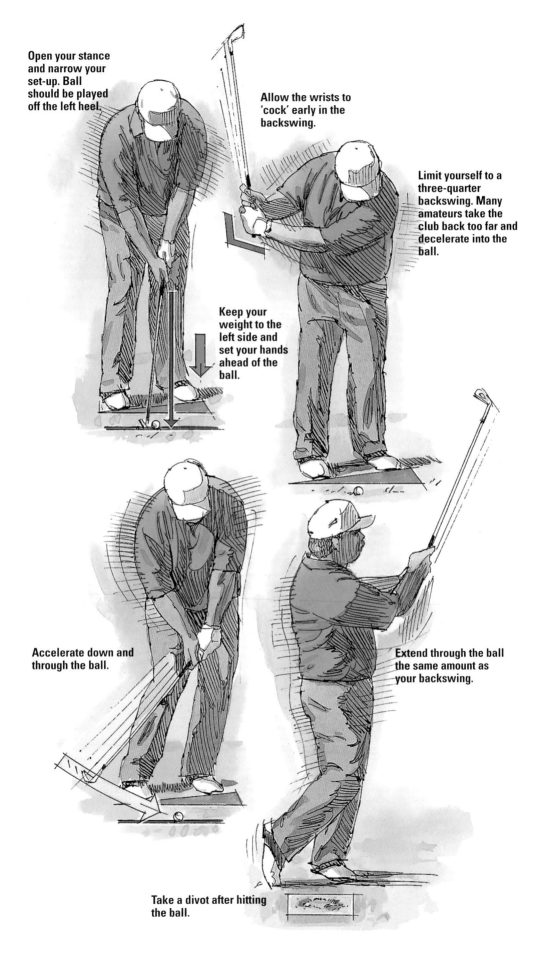

Open your stance and narrow your set-up. Ball should be played off the left heel.

Allow the wrists to 'cock' early in the backswing.

Limit yourself to a three-quarter backswing. Many amateurs take the club back too far and decelerate into the ball.

Keep your weight to the left side and set your hands ahead of the ball.

Accelerate down and through the ball.

Extend through the ball the same amount as your backswing.

Take a divot after hitting the ball.

Stroke Basics

Putting is often called the 'great equalizer' in golf. With skill in this part of your game, the short hitter can outscore the long-ball hitter, the weak can outscore the strong, and the older player can be the equal of the younger.

Good putting is a combination of three prime ingredients, namely, proper stroke basics, sound judgment, and confidence. Once you master the first two, the third will quickly follow.

First Fundamental: Keep it Square

Regardless of which stroke method you prefer, remember the first fundamental in putting. ***The putter is stroked straight back and straight through the target line with the putter face square to that desired line.***

Stance: Assume a square stance, with the feet close together (3 to 12 inches apart), at right angles to the hole. Check your alignment in practice by laying a club down parallel to your feet.

Grip: Although there are many variations, the most common with the pros is the 'reverse overlap grip'. All the fingers of the right hand are on the shaft while the left forefinger rests over the last three fingers of the right hand.

Stroke Methods:

- **Wrist Method:** Little or no arm or shoulder movement. This requires a delicate touch so it is not too popular with the majority of touring pros.

- **Arm and Shoulder Method:** No wrist break. The stroke pivots around the back of the neck.

- **Combination Method:** Most popular on the tour. The arms move with a slight wrist break in the stroke. This is a swing in miniature with the clubface accelerating through contact, always square to the target line.

Whatever method you prefer, avoid collapsing the left wrist at impact. This fault will cause you to pull your putts left of the target.

PUTTING POINTER: Remember the 'square' principle. Don't open or close the clubface at any time in the stroke. Keep it square.

A good way to practice this is to lay two clubs on the practice green 4 or 5 feet from the hole. Line them up parallel to the hole – 5 inches apart. Practice stroking the ball without hitting the clubs with the putter blade.

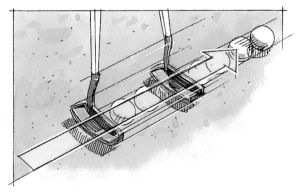

Groove your stroke straight back and straight through the impact area with the clubface square to the target line.

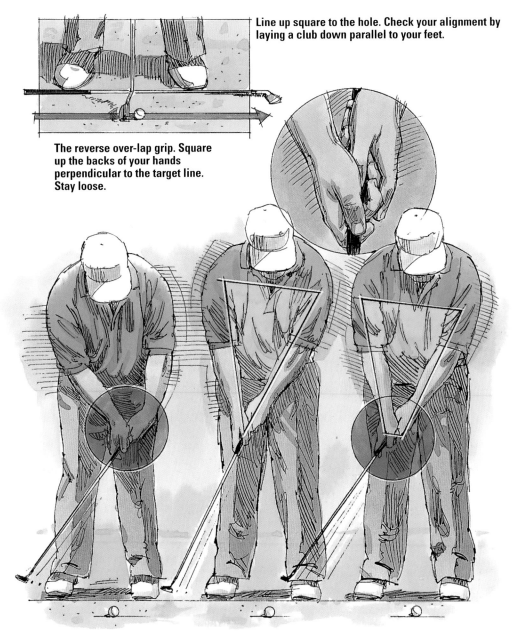

Line up square to the hole. Check your alignment by laying a club down parallel to your feet.

The reverse over-lap grip. Square up the backs of your hands perpendicular to the target line. Stay loose.

Wrist Method: Little or no shoulder or arm movement.

Arm and Shoulder Method: Popular on the tour. The arms, shoulders, and putter stay 'fixed' throughout the swing. No wrist action.

Combination Method: Another popular method. The arms and shoulders move with some wrist action.

Develop a Routine

You can avoid many 'three-putt' greens if you develop a putting routine and stick to it

1. Note the general slope of the green while approaching it.

2. Note the speed of the greens (either on the practice green or by watching others putt).

3. When checking the break of your putt, pick a spot on the green other than the cup, i.e., a brown spot, cleat mark, etc., and line up on it. Don't change your mind over the putt.

4. Take a couple of practice stokes to reinforce the correct swing weight to the hole.

5. Square your stance, feet parallel to the target line.

6. Set your putter face behind the ball square to the target line, at right angles to your feet.

7. Stroke the ball, with the clubface square and the swing motion straight back and straight through the target line.

8. On all putts, follow through the putt with the clubface still square to the hole. Accelerate into and past the ball.

Always study the slope of the green while approaching it.

On breaking putts, pick a spot on the initial line of the putt and make it your target.

Set your putter blade square to your target line before taking your stance. With the putter square, take your stance parallel to the line.

Remember to keep the putter blade square to the target. Swing straight back and accelerate into the ball.

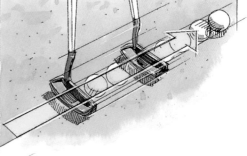

Only practice and experience can improve this part of your game. Keep the following fundamentals in mind when judging your putts or chips.

Grain: The term 'grain' is simply the direction in which the grass grows. This can be determined by looking for the 'shine' or 'sheen' of the putting surface. When the green reflects the sun and appears brighter, you are looking down grain. Putts down grain, or with the grain, will run faster.

Another method of determining grain is to stroke your putter in the fringe just off the putting surface. Fringe grass usually has the same grain as the green.

Remember	
Putting	**Ball Will**
With the grain	Run faster
Against the grain	Run slower
When the grain is in the direction of the cross-slope	Break more than normal
When the grain is against the direction of the cross-slope	Break less than normal
Downhill with the grain	Run faster and break less
Uphill against the grain	Run slower and break more

Contour: When walking to the green, study the general slope of the land. Most greens on flat courses are built higher at the back and lower to the front. When putting from the front of such greens, the putt will be uphill, from the back, downhill. Any putt across such a green will usually break toward the front or lower portion of the surface.

Many pros use the 'plumb-bob' technique to detect the direction and degree of break. (see Plumb-bobbing, chapter 24)

On long approach putts, the common tendency for high handicappers is to concentrate too much on the break and too little on 'pace' or speed. Once you decide on a line, think 'distance' as your primary swing thought.

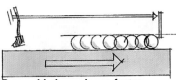

Putts with the grain run faster.

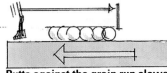

Putts against the grain run slower.

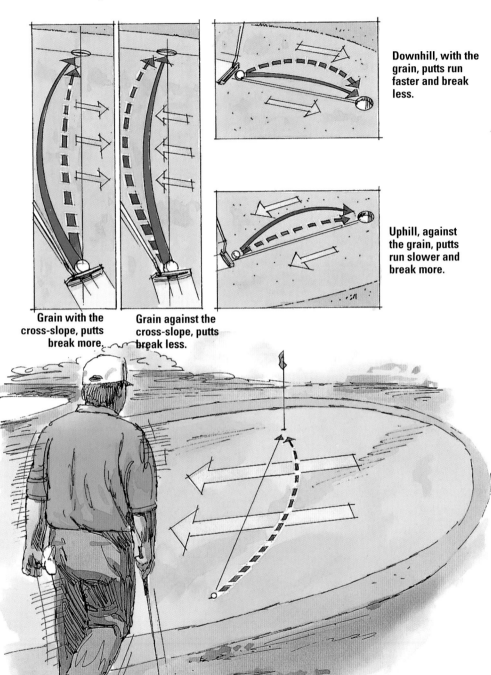

Downhill, with the grain, putts run faster and break less.

Uphill, against the grain, putts run slower and break more.

Grain with the cross-slope, putts break more.

Grain against the cross-slope, putts break less.

Always study the slope of the green as you walk to it. Often the grass growing on the fringe will indicate the direction the grain is growing.

Tips for Short Putts

Missing three-foot putts is one of the most frustrating 'mind-burners' in golf. Understanding the most common causes of problems in this critical area of your game will help you cure those short putt woes.

Common Causes and Cures: Short putts are often missed simply because the player lets up on the stroke before or at impact. Remember that three footers are like any other putt. ***Stroke through the ball. Do not decelerate into the ball, stroke it.***

If alignment is your problem, focus on keeping the putterhead square to the line through the backswing, at impact, and during the follow-through.

On breaking three footers, there isn't much distance for the ball to break appreciably. Therefore, do not give up the cup. ***In other words, unless the slope is severe, don't aim the ball outside the hole.***

Tips for the Short Ones

Aim for a Spot: When missing short putts is causing havoc in your game, ***aim for a spot along the proper line and stroke the ball towards it.*** Follow through with the putterhead moving towards the selected spot.

Increase your Backswing: If your nerves are being frayed, try increasing your backswing slightly and stroking easier. Again, don't quit at the ball. Stroke through the ball.

Lighten up on the Grip: Many golfers unconsciously grip the putter tighter when faced with a short putt. ***Decrease grip pressure considerably.*** This will help keep the putter square to the target and eliminate pushed and pulled putts.

Do not Freeze over the Putt: Don't let yourself become tensed up by standing over a short putt for an eternity. ***Follow your routine.*** Once you decide on line and speed, take a couple of practice strokes. Assume your stance, set the putter 'square' to the line and sink it. Don't wait-stroke.

PRACTICE TIP: Always practice a few short ones before a round of golf. Increase your accuracy by putting to a tee stuck in the green. The hole will seem huge once you are on the golf course.

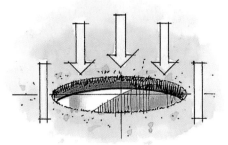

Unless the slope is severe, don't 'give up' the hole. Aim inside the cup.

Reinforce your alignment by picking a spot on the target line and run the ball over that spot.

If you tense up, try increasing the length of your backswing and accelerate through the impact area, square to the hole.

Increase your short putt accuracy. Practice by hitting short putts to a tee in the green. Hitting the tee will make the hole seem huge when playing a round.

Making Long Putts

When faced with a 30 or 40 footer, think of breaking your game plan into two distinct parts. *First, plan the shot, studying the slope, break, etc.* This part of the preparation determines direction. *Once over the ball, think execution,* focusing on distance not direction.

First the planning…

On all putts, do your homework. Study the greens with particular attention to the overall slope of the putting surface and the individual breaks on the putting line. Pay attention to the grain and other factors that may influence your stroke.

Once you have studied the green, decide on the proper target line. Pick a spot on the target line a few feet in front of your ball and set your alignment on it. Assume a square stance, feet parallel to the target line, putterface square to the target.

Now the execution…

All the mental preparation to this point has been direction. *The execution part of the plan stresses distance.* Remember that it is more likely that you will be 15 feet short or past the hole, than being 15 feet left or right.

Once over the ball, concentrate on the speed of the putt. *Think distance only.*

Take a couple of practice strokes and visualize the ball crossing over your selected 'spot' and running up to the hole.

On 50 footers, think of playing to a *three foot circle* around the hole.

On sloping greens, play all long approach shots so that your second putt is uphill. This will lessen the number of 'downhillers'.

Missing to the Left: If you continually miss to the left on long putts, you are probably collapsing your left wrist at impact and closing the putterface. *Remember the first fundamental of the putting stroke.* The putter is stroked straight back and straight through the target line, keeping the putterface square to the desired line.

PRACTICE POINTERS: On long putts, check the squareness of your alignment by assuming your stance then laying a club parallel to your feet. The club should point to a spot approximately one foot to the left of the pin.

On the practice green, stroke the majority of your putts from within 15 feet of the hole. These are the ones you will face most often on the course.

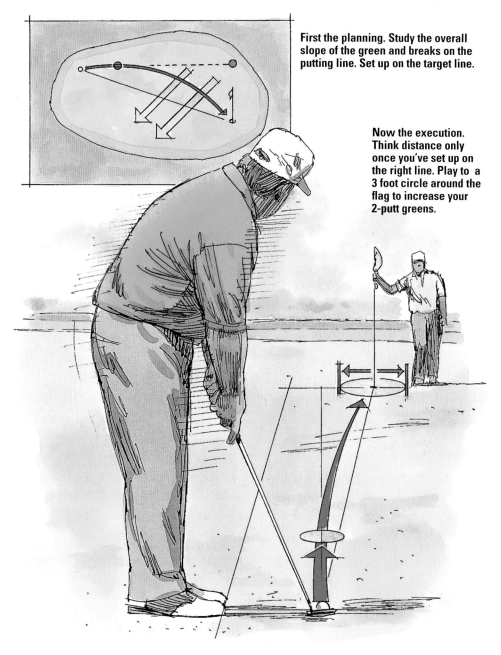

First the planning. Study the overall slope of the green and breaks on the putting line. Set up on the target line.

Now the execution. Think distance only once you've set up on the right line. Play to a 3 foot circle around the flag to increase your 2-putt greens.

On the practice green, lay a club down parallel to your stance to check your alignment. Setting up square will eliminate one variable in an already difficult shot.

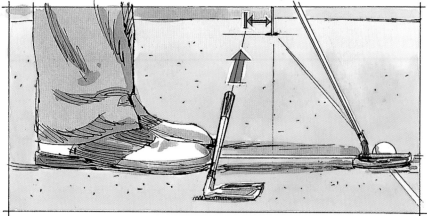

The 'Texas' Wedge

The putter or so-called 'Texas wedge' is usually the safest club to use when your ball is just off the green. Using a putter in this situation will give more consistent results than hitting a 9 iron or pitching wedge. The slightest miscue with the higher-lofted clubs will result in the ball being 'flubbed' an embarrassing foot or two.

Your worst putt will generally be as good as your best chip.

There are situations when you can use the Texas wedge from well off the green. If there's short, closely cropped fringe, you can hit the putter from a considerable distance. Depending on the lie, the putter can be used from green-side bunkers providing there is no lip to contend with. Use your imagination!

When to Putt	When to Chip
short fringe grass	thicker, longer fringe
with the grain	against the grain
good lie	poor lie
no bumpy terrain	uneven, bumpy surface

Planning the Shot: As with any long putt, study the slope, break, etc. Pay attention to the grain and any other factors that may influence your stroke. Pick a spot on the edge of the green on the proper target line and assume your normal putting stance, with the putterface square to the selected line.

Executing the Shot: Avoid making the mistake of trying to 'loft' the ball over the fringe. This will usually result in the putter hitting the grass before the ball.

Play the shot with your hands slightly ahead of the ball. Stroke the putter crisply and slightly downward into the ball. The ball should 'pop' off the putter and bounce a couple of feet.

PRACTICE POINTER: Confidence with the 'Texas Wedge' comes with practice. The downward stroke into the ball decreases distance from a normal putt, so adjust the force of the stroke accordingly.

Putting from just off the green is more consistent than pitching or chipping. Pick a spot on the target line and set up square to that point.

Play your normal putting stroke. Stroke the putter crisply and slightly downward into the ball.

Hitting slightly downward will 'pop' the ball a foot or two and run to the hole. Allow for less roll than a normal putt.

Plumb-bobbing

This technique is employed by many scratch golfers to help determine the direction and amount of break in a putt as well as the general slope of the green.

First, you must determine what eye is 'dominant'. Simply extend your arm and look at a small object a few feet away through a circle formed by your thumb and forefinger. Alternately, close your eyes, one at a time. ***The object will appear to remain in the circle when your dominant eye is open and will appear to jump out of the circle when your dominant eye is closed.***

To judge slope and break, simply squat five or six feet behind your ball as you would when normally lining up a putt and allow the putter to hang freely between your thumb and forefinger. Move your arm so that the club's shaft appears to cut through the center of the ball (sighted with your dominant eye).

If the hole appears to the left of the shaft, the break is from right to left.

If the hole appears to the right, the break is from left to right.

If the shaft appears in the center of the hole, the ball should not break in either direction. Hit it straight.

Determine your 'dominant' eye. Alternately close your eyes. The flag will remain in the circle with the dominant eye and 'pop' out of the circle with the weaker one.

Allow the club to 'hang' freely.

Hole to the left means the putt will break left.

Hole to the right means the putt will break right.

Hole in the center means a straight putt.

The Pinehurst Clubhouse,
Pinehurst, NC

Craig Stadler's Complete Golf Desk Reference

Instant Index

Alignment Problems

Problem Description: The ball is hit solidly without slicing or hooking yet travels consistently to the right or left of the target.

Common Causes:

- Improper stance

- Improper shoulder alignment

- Assumption of stance before target selection

Correcting Misalignment: Pros and amateurs alike sometimes have problems with poor alignment. If your shots are chronically off target even though you feel your alignment is correct, try the following.

- **Check your stance.** On all full shots, your stance should be square. After you have addressed the ball, drop a club by your feet and set it parallel to your toes. If the club points to the right, that is the direction you will hit the shot. Try this drill on the practice range until proper alignment becomes second nature.

- **Check your shoulder alignment.** Many golfers align their shoulders to point directly at the flag. This will cause misalignment to the right. Line up your shoulders to a target *left* of the flagstick, *parallel to the line* from your ball to the hole.

- **Select target before assuming your stance.** Another common cause of poor alignment is to set up over the ball before deciding on a target. Start your preparation by standing behind your ball and looking towards the target. Once you decide on your line, *pick a spot (divot, leaf etc.)* a few feet in front of your ball on the target line. *Assume your stance parallel to the imaginary line* between your ball and the selected spot.

If your shots continue to be 'off-line,' check to see if you are moving your clubface from the square position in the final set-up. *Remember to keep it square.*

If this does not solve the problem, read the sections on 'pushed' and 'pulled' shots.

26

Lay a club parallel to your toes to check your alignment. Club should point to the target.

Line up your shoulders on a line parallel to the line from your ball to the hole.

Always decide on a target before assuming your stance. Pick a spot (leaf or divot) on an imaginary line to the target and set up parallel to the line.

Fat Shots

Problem Description: Hitting a fat shot or 'chunking' is simply hitting the ground before the ball. Many golfers suffer a mild form of chunking without realizing it. Their shots lack distance as well as bite on the green, caused by failure to impart backspin on the ball at impact.

Common Causes:

- Crouching too low at address
- Jerky, chopping swing
- Hitting off the right side with no weight shift
- Faulty leg and hip action
- Head movement downward or to the right on the downswing
- Dropped right shoulder on the downswing

Curing Fat Shots: Fat shots can be eliminated by improving your overall swing pattern. The two most common reasons for fat shots are ***head movement*** during the swing and a ***jerky swing*** with improper weight transfer.

- **Check your address:** If you crouch too much at address, try standing more erect.

- **Check for head movement:** Excessive head movement downward and to the right on the downswing is a primary cause of the 'fat' shot. ***Downward head movement will cause the right shoulder to drop*** resulting in clubhead contact with the ground behind the ball. Read section 29 to eliminate excessive head movement.

- **Lead the downswing with a lateral hip slide:** A common cause of hitting fat is a jerky, arms only swing. The golfer chops down into the ball. Concentrate on hitting through the ball by leading the downswing with a ***lateral hip slide*** towards the target. This will properly transfer your weight through the impact area.

Fat shots can be caused by hitting off the right side with no weight shift.

Fat shots are caused by the club hitting the ground behind the ball.

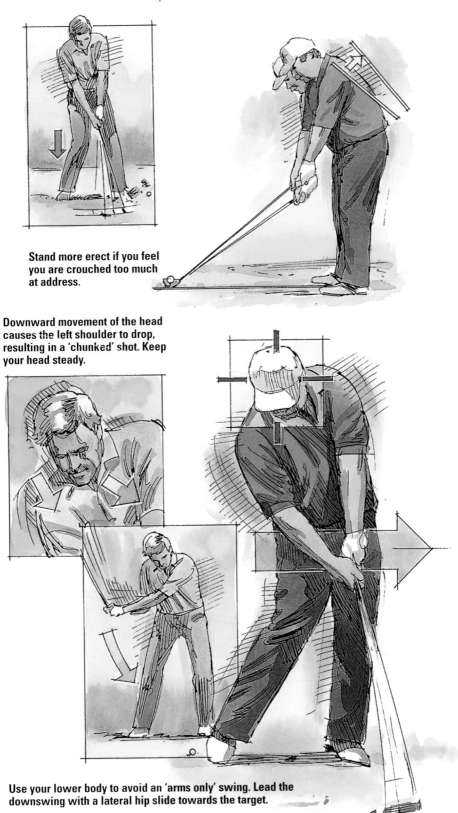

27

Stand more erect if you feel you are crouched too much at address.

Downward movement of the head causes the left shoulder to drop, resulting in a 'chunked' shot. Keep your head steady.

Use your lower body to avoid an 'arms only' swing. Lead the downswing with a lateral hip slide towards the target.

First Tee Jitters

Nothing is more discouraging to an enjoyable game of golf than letting first-tee jitters destroy your first shot. The key, obviously, is to relax. Yet, for many golfers, a relaxed start to the game is often difficult to achieve.

Try the following steps to remove this element from your game.

- **Warm up.** It is always amazing to see golfers go the first tee directly from the club storage area, or car, without **any** warm-up. A few simple words of advice here. **Never go to the first tee without finishing a warm-up routine**. Start on the practice green. Get your putting stroke in the groove by practice putting a few balls. Hit a few balls on the practice range starting with the wedge, ending with a few woods. If this is impossible, push a tee into the ground (away from the teeing area) and warm up by swinging the club over an imaginary ball. **Concentrate on swinging in a smooth rhythmical arc.** Emphasize a slow, deliberate takeback of the club from the tee.

- Get into the habit of checking your grip, stance, alignment, head sway, etc. during the practice session.

- Over the ball, assume your stance in a relaxed, unhurried manner. Do not rush the shot in an attempt to get it over with. **Many of the touring pros take a couple of deep breaths when tension creeps into this part of their game.**

Swing Basics: Always waggle the club behind the ball to start the swing sequence. **The single most important factor is starting with a smooth, rhythmical swing with a slow, deliberate takeaway.** On the backswing, concentrate on a *'low'* and *'slow'* start to the swing.

> Your primary swing thought should be to *relax your forearms and shoulders* during the first couple of shots. *Avoid trying to overpower the shot.* Concentrate, rather, on making solid contact with the ball with an unhurried, relaxed swing.

Start your warm-up routine by putting for 5 or 10 minutes.

Try to start every round by hitting a bucket on the practice range. Start with easy wedges and work up to your driver.

28

If there is no practice range, push a tee into the ground away from the teeing area and warm up by swinging over the tee. Swing with a couple of irons to limber up.

Always 'waggle' the club to start the swing sequence.

Think of relaxing your shoulders and forearms on the first tee. Start with a smooth, rhythmical swing well within your power. Start it 'low and slow'.

Problem Description: Excessive lateral sway of the head and upper body during the swing can cause all sorts of problems, including countless mishits and, most commonly, loss of distance.

Common Causes:

- Trying for extra distance
- Faulty knee action

Curing Excessive Head Movement: It is important to understand why it is absolutely essential to avoid excessive head movement during the swing.

The head is the center or fulcrum of the swing. Around the head, the body coils like a spring during the backswing, then unleashes on the downswing and follow-through. Any lateral head movement will weaken the shot and introduce several variables into an already complicated swing.

Head movement up and down is a frequent cause of fat shots and whiffs.

Try the following tips to eliminate head sway from your game.

- **Center the swing around your chin.** Many pros use this bit of advice when excessive lateral sway creeps into their shot making. ***Keep a steady head*** by thinking of pointing your chin at the ball at address. Keep your chin in place through impact.

- **Keep your knees flexed.** Sway can be caused by faulty knee action. Trying to get extra distance on a shot can cause the player to overswing when the clubhead is taken back. This lifts the head and straightens the knees. ***Keep the knees flexed*** and try hitting flat-footed, without lifting your left heel off the ground.

PRACTICE POINTER: *Watch your shadow.* **Perhaps the easiest way to correct excessive head sway is to practice swinging with the sun behind your back. Line your shadow up to a spot on the grass then watch for any lateral or vertical sway during the swing. Study the 'feel' of your head remaining steady at the center of the swing arc.**

Avoid excessive head movement. Think of centering your swing around your head. Point your chin at the ball and swing around it.

29

Keep your knees flexed. Excessive head movement can be caused by over-swinging and straightening the knees on the backswing.

Swing with the sun behind your back. Watch your shadow for any excessive head movement laterally or vertically.

Hits on the Toe

Problem Description: At impact, the clubface contacts the ball on the toe of the club, causing a definite loss of distance. The shot often pulls to the left of the target line.

Common Causes:

- Standing too far from the ball
- Ball position too far forward
- Excessive hip spin on the downswing

Correcting Hits on the Toe: Most golfers occasionally hit a mid or long iron shot off the toe of the club. If your problem is a chronic one, check the following pointers to help eliminate this mishit.

- **Check your set-up.** Toed hits are commonly caused by **_reaching too far_** for the ball. Reaching too far for the ball will also give a golfer a 'flat' swing plane and cause the ball to slice.

- **At address, sole the club flat on the ground.** Center your clubface behind the ball. **_Assume a fairly upright posture,_** with your hands no more than six inches from your body. This set-up encourages a more vertical swing plane.

- **Check your ball position.** Some golfers play the **_ball too far forward_** in their address. This causes contact with the ball when the clubhead is returning inside the target line. If this applies to your set up, **_try moving the ball more inside the left heel._**

- **Excessive hip swing.** A common cause of toed hits is an excessive hip swing on the downswing. This can be corrected by mentally stressing **_lateral hip slide_** along the target line on the downswing.

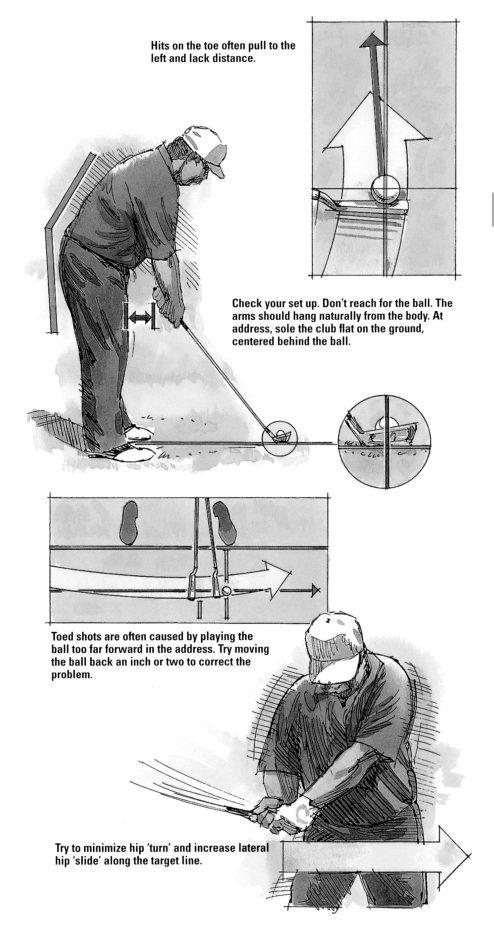

Hits on the toe often pull to the left and lack distance.

30

Check your set up. Don't reach for the ball. The arms should hang naturally from the body. At address, sole the club flat on the ground, centered behind the ball.

Toed shots are often caused by playing the ball too far forward in the address. Try moving the ball back an inch or two to correct the problem.

Try to minimize hip 'turn' and increase lateral hip 'slide' along the target line.

Problem Description: A hooked ball usually travels low and curves to the left for right-handed golfers. The ball rolls farther than the straight shot. For this reason, the 'draw,' a hook in miniature, is one of the strongest shots in the game.

Common Causes:

- Improper 'strong' grip (common)
- Closed stance
- Flat 'horizontal' swing plane
- Crossing the line. The club points right of the target at the top of the backswing
- Poor shoulder alignment (to the right of target)

Curing the Hook: To eliminate the hook from your game, understand the basic underlying problem in your swing.

The hook results from a **'closed' clubface** contacting the ball on a definite **inside-to-outside swing path.** This imparts **'counterclockwise' side-spin** to the ball. Golfers who hook chronically align farther and farther to the right and compound the problem.

To cure your hook, concentrate on three main areas of your swing, namely: **grip, stance, and swing plane.**

- **Check your grip.** The most common cause of a hook is a 'strong' grip. The right hand is positioned too far under the shaft at address. At impact, the wrists rotate to the left and 'close' the clubface. Weaken your grip (see section 1 on proper grip). **The 'V' of the right hand should point to the right shoulder.**

- **Check your stance and alignment.** A closed stance will produce an 'inside-to-outside' swing path. Assume a square stance with the shoulders and hips parallel to the target line.

- **Swing more vertically.** A swing plane that is too flat will cause a hooked shot. Swing more vertically with the straight left arm pointing down into the ball at the top of your swing. Point the club at the target at the top of the backswing.

Drawing the ball is one of the strongest shots in golf, and probably the most difficult to master. Close your stance slightly to the target line. *Keep the clubface square to the target.* This will close the face slightly to the actual 'inside-to-outside' swing path. Take a normal swing and the club should impart a slight side-spin to the ball. Don't try this one on the course without a lot of practice.

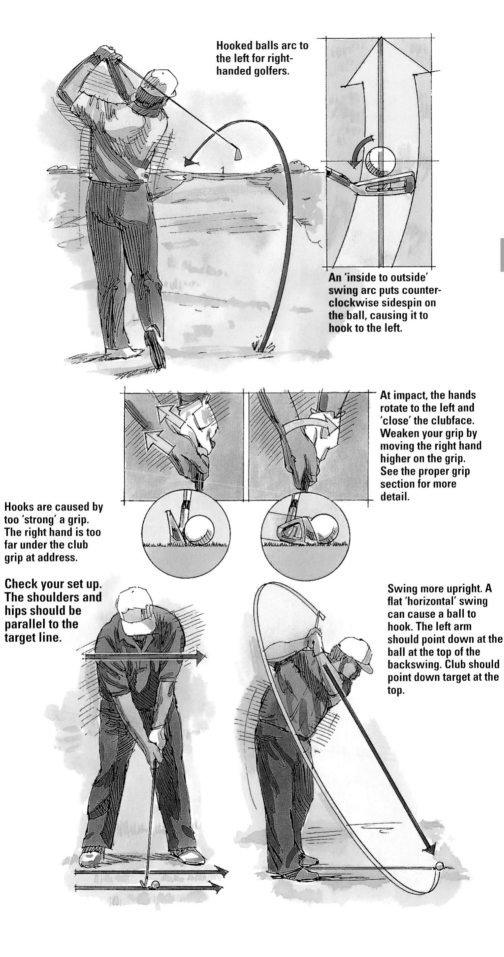

Hooked balls arc to the left for right-handed golfers.

31

An 'inside to outside' swing arc puts counter-clockwise sidespin on the ball, causing it to hook to the left.

At impact, the hands rotate to the left and 'close' the clubface. Weaken your grip by moving the right hand higher on the grip. See the proper grip section for more detail.

Hooks are caused by too 'strong' a grip. The right hand is too far under the club grip at address.

Check your set up. The shoulders and hips should be parallel to the target line.

Swing more upright. A flat 'horizontal' swing can cause a ball to hook. The left arm should point down at the ball at the top of the backswing. Club should point down target at the top.

Problem Description: A jerky swing is often difficult to self-diagnose. Many times, your golf partners may comment on the problem by telling you that you have 'lunged' at the shot or that your swing is 'too fast'. Trying to 'kill' the ball is probably the most common expression.

Common Causes:

- Trying for maximum distance
- Tension
- Over-swinging

Cure: Golfers who are prone to a 'jerky' swing would do well to remember two fundamental rules.

1. Contacting the ball squarely is as important as clubhead speed for distance.

2. The slower the backswing, the greater the distance a ball will fly.

Try the following to eliminate the jerky swing from your game.

- **Start with a waggle and press.** The worst way to start a swing is from a frozen, static position. All scratch golfers introduce some sort of movement before starting the backswing. *Waggle the club a few times* to set yourself up for a smooth start.

- **Start slowly.** Do not make the cardinal mistake of trying for more distance by quickly jerking the club away from the ball on the backswing. A fast take-away will virtually destroy any chance of making a good shot. *Take the club back slowly and deliberately.* The first few inches should be ridiculously slow. This will enhance a square clubhead at impact and give you greater distance.

- **Avoid the urge to kill.** Smoothness, rhythm, and square clubhead at impact will do more for distance than any attempt to 'power' the ball an extra 20 yards. Watch the touring pros on the next televised tournament. The great majority rely on a smooth, fluid swing for distance and accuracy.

- **Relax forearms and shoulders.** Try keeping tension from your swing by concentrating on this swing thought.

Practice hitting a bucket of balls, staying well within your capabilities, concentrating on square impact over clubhead speed. Try hitting a few ridiculously slowly. The distance the ball will fly will surprise you.

Start your swing with a waggle and forward press. This eliminates a frozen, static start to the swing.

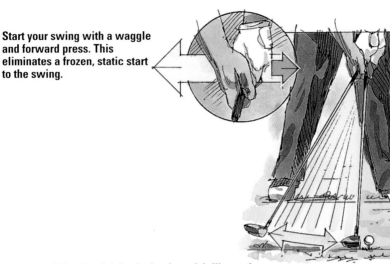

32

Take the club back slowly and deliberately. Keep your shoulders and forearms loose and relaxed.

SLOW

Concentrate on hitting it square, staying well within your capabilities. Avoid the urge to 'kill' the ball. When practicing, work on a smooth, fluid swing finishing with a high classic finish.

Loss of Balance (Spinning Out)

Problem Description: Loss of balance during the follow-through is often referred to as 'spinning out' of the shot. In order to prevent falling forward after impact, the golfer takes a quick step with his or her right foot towards the target. Slices and pulled shots usually result from this type of swing error.

Common Causes:

- Lateral head sway
- Overreaching for the ball—weight on the toes
- Failure to keep weight inside
- Raising the right heel prematurely

Curing Poor Balance: Without good balance, consistency in distance and direction is impossible.

- **Avoid lateral head sway.** This is a common cause of 'spinning out' of a shot. The head moves towards the target on the downswing, resulting in horizontal shoulder movement to the left. The resulting 'flat' swing invites a slice. ***Keep your head steady throughout the swing.***

- **Do not overreach for the ball.** If you find yourself on your toes in the impact zone, you are probably reaching for the ball. To make contact, you tend to stretch forward and lose your balance. Check your stance. ***Keep your weight back on the heels.*** At address, plant your weight just ahead of your heels.

- **Keep your weight inside.** Do not allow your weight to drift outside your left foot on the downswing. ***Think of flexing your knees and 'sitting down'*** on the ball throughout the swing.

- **Delay your right heel rise.** Spinning out of a shot is sometimes caused by prematurely allowing the right heel to lift on the downswing. ***Try rolling the ankles, pushing off the right heel on the downswing.*** Keep it firmly planted on the ground.

An effective swing thought to prevent 'spinning out' of a shot is to concentrate on swinging in a more vertical plane and finishing high. Try to copy the finish of touring pros on televised tournaments.

Loss of balance is caused by lateral head movement towards the target. The golfer 'spins out' of the shot causing the ball to slice or pull.

33

The head is the center or fulcrum of the swing. Avoid excessive head movement by anchoring the swing around the chin.

Do not overreach for the ball. Set up with the arms hanging naturally from the body, knees flexed, and back slightly bent.

If you overreach for the ball, your weight will be on your toes. Keep your weight to the inside, and centered on your feet.

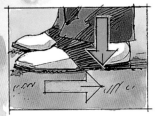

Delay the rise of your right heel. Instead of lifting your right heel, try rolling the ankles, pushing off the right heel on the downswing.

Low Drives (Smothered Shots)

Problem Description: With the driver, fairway woods, and long irons, the ball is struck solidly yet barely gets off the ground. The club strikes the ball in a closed position, decreasing the effective loft of the clubface.

Common Causes:

- Improper grip
- Ball teed too low (driver)
- Ball position too far back in stance
- Hands too far ahead at address

Curing Smothered Shots: Golfers who consistently hit low or 'smothered' shots are decreasing the natural built-in loft of the club being used. Check your grip and address in the following manner.

- **Check your grip.** A strong grip closes the clubface at impact. With a strong grip, 3 or 4 knuckles of the left hand are visible at address. During impact, the hands and wrists rotate counterclockwise and close the clubface even further. ***Remember the two knuckle rule.*** Two knuckles of the left hand should be visible at address. If an improper grip is causing you to smother your shots, reread the section on proper grip.

- **Tee the ball higher.** When using the driver, tee the ball so that ***one-half*** of the ball is above the clubhead.

- **Check the ball position at address.** You should play the ball off your left heel for the driver and one to two inches inside the left heel for the long irons.

- **Check your hand position.** The hands should be even with the ball at address with most shots. The shaft and left arm should form a straight line to the ball.

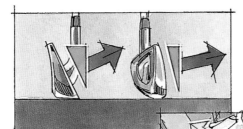

Low drives and smothered shots are caused by the club striking the ball in a closed or hooded position.

Too strong a grip can smother a shot. At impact, the hands and wrists rotate counterclockwise and close the clubface.

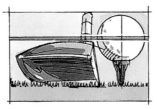

With a strong grip, three or four knuckles of the left hand are visible at address. Correct with the 'two knuckle' rule.

Tee up the ball so that one-half of the ball is above the clubhead.

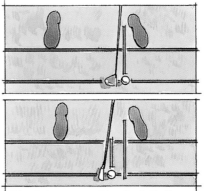

34

Check your setup. Play the ball off your left heel for the driver and one to two inches inside the left heel for long irons.

Position your hands so that the shaft and left arm form a straight line to the ball.

Pulled/Pushed Shots

Problem Description: Both pulled and pushed shots are caused by the clubface contacting the ball squarely but with the path of the clubface either right of the desired line (pushed) or left (pulled). Both shots are straight, differentiating them from slices and hooks.

- **A pulled shot** is caused by the clubhead traveling from an *'outside-to-inside'* path (similar to a slice) except that the clubface is square to the swingpath and *'closed'* relative to the intended line of flight.

- **A pushed shot** is the result of an *'inside-to-outside'* swingpath with the clubface square to that direction and *'open'* relative to the intended line of flight.

Common Causes	
Pulled Shots *(left of target)*	**Pushed Shots *(right of target)***
• Strong grip	• Weak grip
• Ball too far forward in stance	• Ball too far back in stance
• Open stance	• Closed stance
• Head and body sway	• Head and body sway
• Poor swing plane	• Incorrect swing plane

Curing Pushed and Pulled Shots: Remember that the basic fundamental in hitting straight shots is to deliver the clubface square to the ball with the clubhead traveling on a path square to the intended line of flight.

- **Check your grip.** Read section 1 on proper grip. *Remember the 'two knuckle' rule.* Two knuckles of the left hand should be visible at address. If you *'pull'* to the left, *'weaken' your grip* by moving your hands slightly 'counterclockwise' on the shaft. If you *'push'* your shots, *move your hands in a clockwise direction.*

- **Check your stance.** Assume a square stance for every full shot. Play the ball inside the left heel.

- **Check for head sway.** The swing coils around the head. Keep it steady.

- **Swing more vertically.** A more upright swing plane will keep the clubhead traveling along the proper path for a longer period. Make a habit of swinging through to the target with good extension.

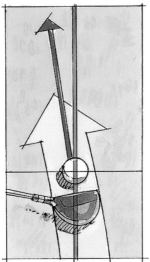

Pulled shot

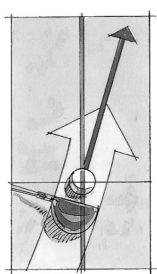

Pushed shot

Straighten your pull by weakening your grip a little by moving your hands 'counter-clockwise' on the shaft.

Straighten your push by moving your hands 'clockwise' a little when you grip the club.

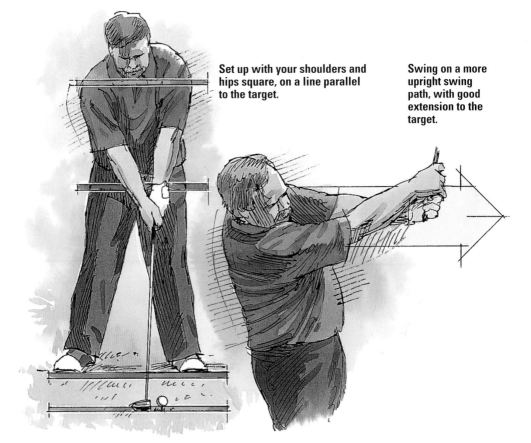

35

Set up with your shoulders and hips square, on a line parallel to the target.

Swing on a more upright swing path, with good extension to the target.

Shanking (Hits on the Heel)

Problem Description: The shank is one of the most destructive swing faults in golf. At impact, the ball contacts the heel or shank of the club and squirts low and to the right of the target line.

Common Causes:

- Standing too close to the ball (common)
- Flattened horizontal swing plane (common)
- Head movement
- Weight 'forward' on the toes at impact
- Backswing too far inside
- Standing too far from the ball (less common)

Curing the Shank: If you have shanking problems, your swing needs major surgery. Understand the mechanics of this swing fault. ***On the downswing, the clubhead is thrown outside the normal swing arc.***

Check the following pointers to try to correct your problem. If this does not help, read the 'swing basics' sections of the book.

- **Check your address.** If you are ***too close*** on the downswing, the arms are forced outside their initial position and a shank occurs.

- **Check your swing plane.** If you are ***too far*** from the ball, the swing plane will be more 'horizontal' than 'vertical'. The shanker tries to adjust and reach for the ball, shifting his weight to the toes. The blade of the club is thrown beyond the ball and a shank results. Don't reach for the ball at address and keep your weight on your heels.

- **Swing more vertically.** Practice taking the clubhead straight back from the ball. Move the left shoulder under the right. If your club points left of the target at the top of the swing, you are guilty of a flat swing. At the top, your left arm should point into the ball, with the club pointing down the target line. Swing through the ball at impact and finish high.

- **Watch for excessive head movement.** If your head doesn't move, the plane of the downswing should be identical to the plane of the backswing. The club shouldn't go outside its normal arc.

Shanking can be caused by a number of factors. The best advice to correct this swing fault is to take a lesson from your local pro.

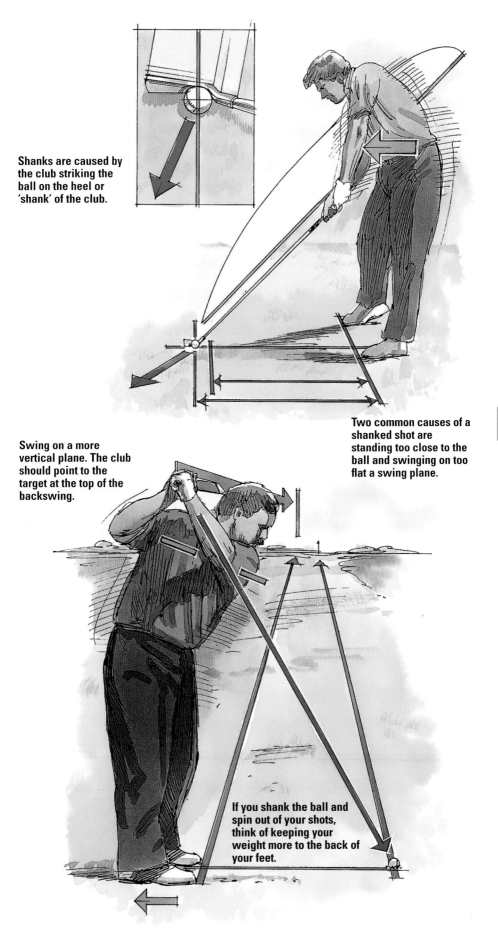

Shanks are caused by the club striking the ball on the heel or 'shank' of the club.

Two common causes of a shanked shot are standing too close to the ball and swinging on too flat a swing plane.

Swing on a more vertical plane. The club should point to the target at the top of the backswing.

36

If you shank the ball and spin out of your shots, think of keeping your weight more to the back of your feet.

Problem Description: The 'pop fly' of golf. The 'skied' shot flies high into the air because the clubhead contacts the ball with too much of the clubface below the ball's center.

Common Causes	
Wood Shots	**Short Irons**
Ball teed too high	Hands behind the ball at impact
Dropping the right shoulder on the downswing	Ball positioned too far forward
Lifting the club too quickly on the backswing, then chopping down on the ball	Weak 'open' grip

Curing Skied Woods: Skied shots are not that difficult to correct if you can identify the cause. Try the following pointers to eliminate the problem.

- **Tee the ball lower.** No more than *one-half* of the ball should rest above the top of the driver head.

- **Keep the backswing 'low and slow'.** Take the clubhead back *slowly with good extension* of the left arm and side.

- **Check for head sway.** Remember that the swing is *centered* around the head. Try pointing your chin at the ball and keeping it there throughout the swing. *Avoid lifting the head* on the backswing.

Curing Skied Short Iron Shots: With the short irons, you are adding unnecessary loft to an already lofted club.

- **Check your grip.** You may be opening the clubface at impact. Strengthen your grip.

- **Check your ball position.** Position the ball two to three inches inside your left heel.

- **Lead your hands into the ball.** If skying short irons is a chronic problem, you may be addressing the ball with your hands *behind* the ball. On the downswing, move your hands well ahead of the club through the impact area.

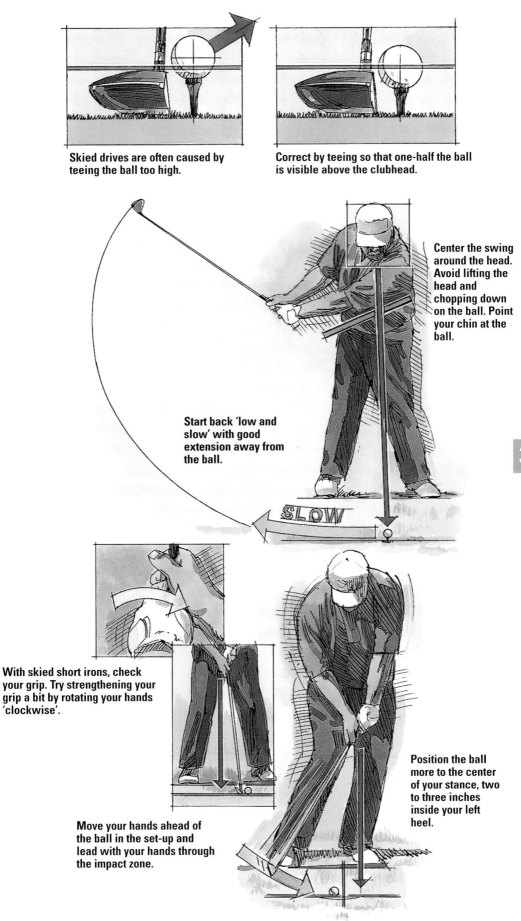

Skied drives are often caused by teeing the ball too high.

Correct by teeing so that one-half the ball is visible above the clubhead.

Center the swing around the head. Avoid lifting the head and chopping down on the ball. Point your chin at the ball.

Start back 'low and slow' with good extension away from the ball.

SLOW

37

With skied short irons, check your grip. Try strengthening your grip a bit by rotating your hands 'clockwise'.

Move your hands ahead of the ball in the set-up and lead with your hands through the impact zone.

Position the ball more to the center of your stance, two to three inches inside your left heel.

Slicing

Problem Description: The slice is one of golf's most common swing faults. The ball curves left to right. Many golfers compensate by aiming more to the left. This can cause more problems by hitting some shots straight left into trouble.

Common Causes	Other Causes
Weak grip	Open clubface at address
Open stance	Strong right hand grip
Poor alignment to the left	Overturning the hips on the downswing
Failure to clear the left side	Over-swinging
Flat 'horizontal' swing plane	Too 'vertical' a swing plane

Curing the Slice: *A slice is caused by an open-faced club coming across the ball from an 'out-to-in' position at impact.* This imparts *'clockwise'* side spin to the ball. With more severe slices, the club is drawn across the ball from well outside the target line with the face of the club open.

To cure your slice, remember this basic rule. *Straight shots result from striking the ball squarely through impact.*

If you slice chronically, the root of your problem likely includes a *poor grip, open stance, and/or a flat swing plane.*

- **Check your grip.** A 'weak' grip promotes an open clubface at impact. Take a stronger grip to help close the face on impact.

- **Check your stance and alignment.** Assume a square stance. Drop a club parallel to your toes and see if the shaft is parallel to the target line. For chronic slicers, the club usually points to the left of the target, causing the shoulders to misalign left. Check the squareness of your clubface at address.

- **Restrict your downswing hip turn.** Try for more lateral hip slide and less turn.

- **Swing more upright.** A flat swing plane promotes slicing. A more vertical plane keeps the clubface on target longer. At the top of the swing, the club should be pointing down the target line.

- **Adjust your swing plane.** Take back your club more to the inside, keeping your left elbow tucked more to the body. This will produce a more 'in-to-out' swing path through impact.

A fade is a controlled slice. The ability to hit a fade is a definite asset and is extremely useful to the low handicapper and pro. Open your stance slightly to the target line. Keep the clubface square to the target. Take a normal swing and the club should impart a slight side-spin to the ball.

Golf's greatest affliction. A sliced ball arcs right for the right-handed golfer.

Slices are caused by an 'outside to inside' swing path that puts 'clockwise' sidespin on the ball.

Strengthen your grip by rotating your hands 'clockwise' on the club.

Set up square with shoulders and hips on a line parallel to the target. Drop a club at your feet after you've taken your stance. Most slicers are pointed well left of the target.

Take the club back more to the inside and start the downswing with less hip turn and more lateral hip slide to the target.

Topping

Problem Description: Topping is defined as hitting the ball above its equator. This can be a devastating problem for the high handicapper. Besides lost distance, almost anything can happen to the shot. 'Whiffing' (missing the ball completely) is an example of this problem at its worst.

Common Causes

- Jerking the head up on the downswing
- Excessive lateral body movement toward the target on the downswing
- Crouching too much at address
- Ball teed too low
- Trying to 'kill' the ball (common cause with low handicappers)

Curing Topped Shots: Most topped shots are the result of changing the swing arc. In other words, the club follows a different path on the downswing than it did on the backswing.

Try to remember that the head is the center of the golf swing. The body coils around this point. Any 'jerking up' of the head at impact will result in a topped shot.

Check the following areas of your swing to remedy your game.

- **Check tee height.** One-half the ball should be visible above the driver.
- **Check your address.** Assume a square stance on all full shots with the ball just inside the left heel. Do not allow yourself to crouch excessively at address.
- **Check for head movement.** A common cause of topped shots is a jerking upward of the head and shoulders at impact. ***Think of your body uncoiling around the head. Concentrate on a smooth relaxed swing through the ball*** versus trying to overpower the shot for extra distance. Check also for excessive 'lateral' head movement left or right. Center the swing around your chin.

Low handicappers sometimes 'cold top' their shots by trying for extra distance. The lateral hip slide is so accelerated that the hands and wrists do not have a chance to release the clubhead into the ball. *Swing well within your capabilities to eliminate this swing fault.*

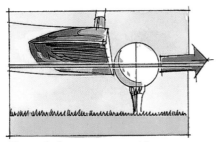

Topped shots are caused by hitting the ball above its equator.

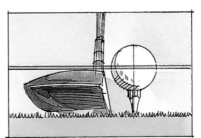

Tee your drives so that one-half the ball is visible above the clubhead.

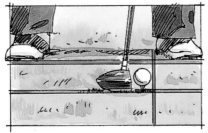

Tee the ball inside the left heel.

Stand more upright if you find yourself crouching too much at address. Too much crouch in the set-up will cause you to compensate by jerking your head up on the downswing and topping the shot.

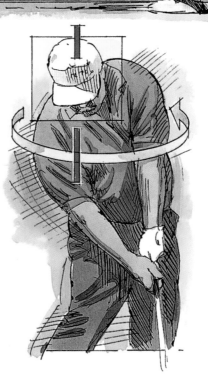

Trying to 'overpower' the shot sometimes causes the head to lift at impact. Center the swing around your head and concentrate on a smooth, relaxed swing.

Hitting a shot from a fairway bunker poses no great problem if the ball has a good lie. Long or middle irons as well as 3, 4, and 5 woods can be used with confidence in this situation. Make the following swing modifications.

Stance: Assume a ***slightly wider and more open stance*** than normal for the club being played. This will minimize body turn and ensures that the clubhead contacts the ball before the sand. Work your shoes into the sand for better footing.

Address: Choke down on the clubshaft to adjust for the wider stance and 'buried' feet. Play the ball one to two inches back from its normal position.

Swing Basics: Take a normal swing being careful not to ground the club. (2 stroke penalty) ***Do not try to overpower the shot.*** The ideal swing 'picks' the ball out cleanly. Aim left of the target and play a fade. Any contact with the sand before the ball will ruin the shot.

Club Selection: Because the 'pivot' or body turn is restricted, 'over-club' one club to adjust for the loss of distance.

HERE'S A TIP FOR MID TO HIGH HANDICAPPERS.

When faced with a long bunker shot, use a fairway wood in preference to an iron. There is less chance of digging into the sand with these flat bottomed clubs.

Remember that any attempt to power the ball out of the bunker will produce an 'explosion' type of shot. The club will strike the sand before the ball and ruin the shot. If anything, hit the ball a little 'thin'.

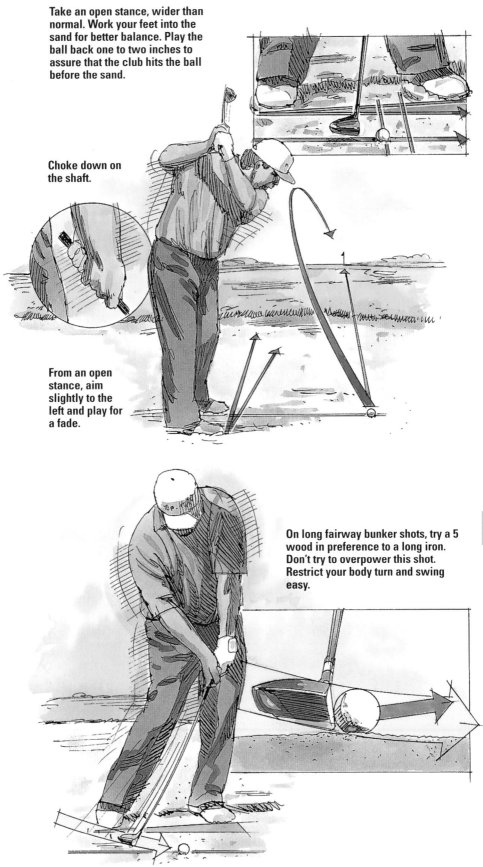

Take an open stance, wider than normal. Work your feet into the sand for better balance. Play the ball back one to two inches to assure that the club hits the ball before the sand.

Choke down on the shaft.

From an open stance, aim slightly to the left and play for a fade.

On long fairway bunker shots, try a 5 wood in preference to a long iron. Don't try to overpower this shot. Restrict your body turn and swing easy.

When hitting from difficult lies, try not to let yourself get 'psyched' up over the prospect of a poor shot. Instead, *take a three-quarter backswing for maximum control* and make the following swing adjustments.

Hard Ground:

- **Ball Position:** In order to insure contact with the ball *before* the hardpan, play the ball farther back in your stance.

- **Shot Basics:** Firm up a little on your grip, keeping your hands *ahead* of the ball at the address position. During the downswing, keep your hands well ahead of the ball. This will further reduce the tendency to hit the hardpan before the ball.

- **Don't try to scoop the ball.** A common fatal mistake is trying to pick the ball from the hardpan. *Be sure to hit down into the ball* and trust the loft of the club to get the shot airborne.

Divot Holes

- **Ball in the center of the divot.** Play a normal shot, making sure to hit down on the ball.

- **Ball resting on the far side of a divot.** Firm up your grip slightly and *close your clubface a little* to prevent the grass catching the toe thus opening the face at impact.

- **Ball resting on near side of a divot.** Firm up your grip slightly and *open your clubface a little* to prevent the grass from catching the heel thus closing the clubface at impact.

Pine Needles

- **Don't ground the club.** Whenever you have to play a ball off of pine needles, be careful not to ground your club. There is a danger the ball will move when you set the club down behind the ball.

- **Chipping the ball.** If the shot calls for a chip, *keep your weight on the left side, and play the ball farther back in your stance.* Play the shot with your hands well forward, making sure your wrists don't collapse at impact.

- **The explosion shot.** If you're greenside, and need loft from pine needles, *play a standard explosion shot* to get the ball over traps, mounds, etc. *Open your stance and clubface.* Take the club up abruptly and swing down and through the ball. Hit an inch behind the ball and follow through to a high finish.

Tensing up will cause more mishits than poor technique. Concentrate on one swing thought for each situation. Keep the arms and shoulders loose and avoid trying to over-power the shot.

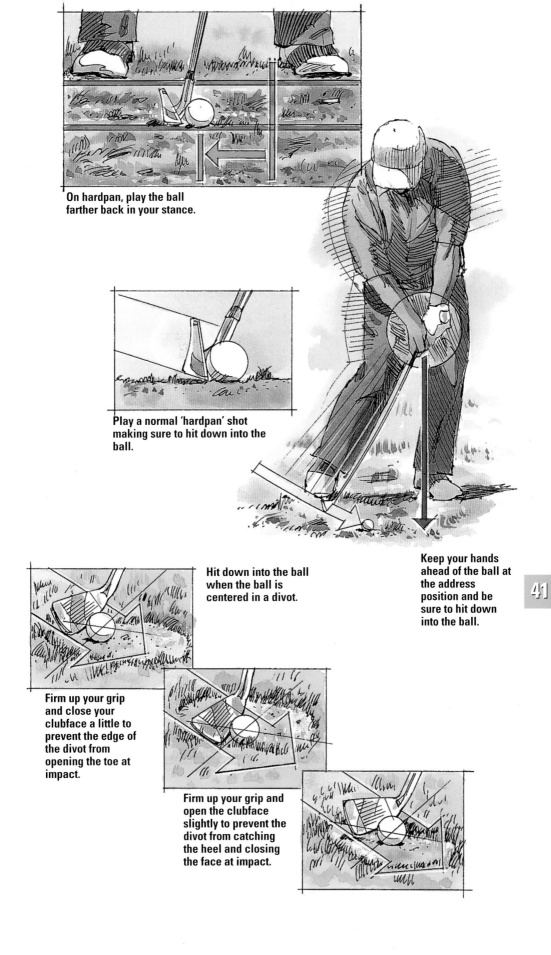

On hardpan, play the ball farther back in your stance.

Play a normal 'hardpan' shot making sure to hit down into the ball.

Hit down into the ball when the ball is centered in a divot.

Keep your hands ahead of the ball at the address position and be sure to hit down into the ball.

41

Firm up your grip and close your clubface a little to prevent the edge of the divot from opening the toe at impact.

Firm up your grip and open the clubface slightly to prevent the divot from catching the heel and closing the face at impact.

When faced with a shot from the rough, *use your head to think your way out of trouble.* The best rule to follow is to play it safe and choose the shot that offers the best recovery with the minimum risk of leaving yourself in an even more difficult situation. *Trying an almost impossible recovery shot seldom succeeds and a double or triple bogey usually follows.*

Treat the rough with the respect it deserves, striving to incorporate the following general guidelines into your recovery strategy.

Club Selection: As a rule, it's better to use a 'more-lofted' club when hitting from the rough. The height of the grass will help dictate your decision. *In higher grass, it is absolutely essential to get maximum loft quickly.*

When distance is required, choose the 4 or 5 wood over the long irons. These 'stroke savers' have greater loft and have less tendency to get caught up in the grass.

Heavy Rough: 'Pop' the ball out of heavy or high rough. Use a well-lofted iron to get the ball back into play.

1. **Assume a slightly open stance.** With a firm grip, choke down on the club one or two inches. Play the ball towards the right foot.

2. **Take the club up more abruptly than usual,** breaking the wrists early. Hit down and through the ball with the hands leading the clubhead.

3. **In heavy rough,** there is a tendency for the grass to wrap around the shaft and close the clubface. Open the blade slightly to compensate.

4. **Do not try to overpower this shot.** The ball will tend to come out flying with little backspin 'bite' on the fairway or green so adjust your shot accordingly.

Light Rough: When distance is required and the lie is fairly decent, choose a versatile 4 or 5 wood over the long irons.

1. **The high trajectory woods can be real 'stroke savers'.** They can 'pop' the ball out and are less likely to be caught up in the grass.

2. **Take a more upright swing** and hit down and through the ball.

Never try for more distance than the lie of your ball indicates. Play it safe.

Obviously, the best way to handle the rough is to stay out of it. Off the tee, *hit away from trouble.* If there is trouble on the left, hit from the left side of the teeing area, giving yourself a maximum angle away from difficulty.

Use a more-lofted club to get maximum loft quickly. 'Pop' the ball out of heavy or high rough.

If you are a mid to high handicapper, choose the 5 wood over a long iron. There is less tendency for the clubhead to get caught up in the grass.

Take the club up more abruptly than a regular shot with the wrists breaking early.

Choke down on the club one to two inches.

Open your stance slightly.

In light rough, take a more upright swing and hit down and through the ball.

In heavy rough, open the clubface slightly. Grass can wrap around the hosel and close the clubface.

42

Success with the explosion shot is simply a matter of sound technique combined with a little practice. Understanding the basic theory behind sand-shot technique will go a long way to improving your bunker play.

Theory behind the Shot: The theory behind virtually every type of sand shot is to ***take a 'slice' of sand from under the ball.*** The sand wedge never strikes the ball directly but slices out an area of sand about the size of a dollar bill. The ball is 'splashed' out of the bunker on a cushion of sand.

Address: Play the explosion shot with an exaggerated **open stance.** The ball should be positioned forward, opposite the left heel.

Open the clubface slightly.

Work your shoes well into the sand to ensure good footing as well as to gain information about the type of sand to be played from.

Choke down on the clubshaft. This prevents the clubhead from digging too deeply.

Swing: Like the pitch, the sand shot swing is mainly an arms, shoulder, and hand shot with little hip movement. The hands 'uncock' early in the swing and 'flick' the ball towards the pin.

On a normal lie, the club slices into the sand approximately two inches behind the ball.

Tempo: Many amateurs tense up and quicken their swing when hitting the sand shot. On the practice range, ***try humming a slow tune*** such as 'Swing low sweet chariot' and swing to that tempo.

Tension and 'stopping at the ball' are the greatest destroyers of effective sand play. Use a smooth, unhurried swing with little tension in the forearms and shoulders.

Do not quit on the ball. Many high handicappers have a tendency to let up at impact. Hit through the ball, driving your hands towards the target.

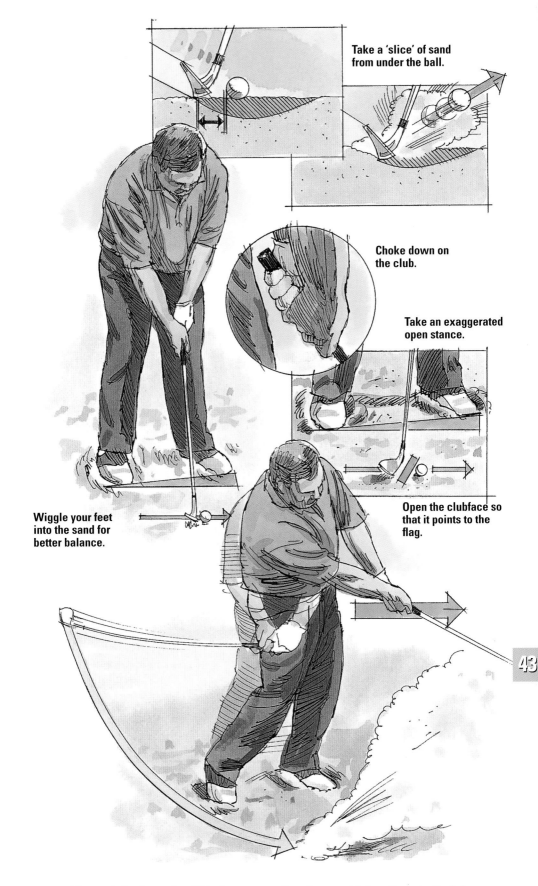

Take a 'slice' of sand from under the ball.

Choke down on the club.

Take an exaggerated open stance.

Open the clubface so that it points to the flag.

Wiggle your feet into the sand for better balance.

43

The sand shot is not that difficult to master. Keep loose and follow through. Cock the wrists early in the backswing and hit down and through the ball. The ball will be 'splashed' out of the bunker on a cushion of sand.

Practice is the key to better sand play. Use the following pointers to build your confidence in bunker play.

Normal Lie: Use the following swing adjustments to play various sand textures.

Sand Type	Impact Behind Ball	Comments
Normal, coarse	two inches	Use the basic explosion shot (section 43).
Wet or moist	one inch	Wedge may bounce. Use a 9 iron. Firm up grip.
Dry or powdery	two to three inches	Club will tend to bury. Use a more forceful swing and follow through.
Artificial sand (silica)	two to three inches	Ball often forms a 'fried egg' lie. Hit the edge of the depression. Square the clubface. Swing more forcefully and follow through.

Buried Lie: Try using your pitching wedge or sand wedge to cut down into the sand. Close the clubface slightly and play the ball off the right foot from a square stance. Hit two to three inches behind the ball *accentuating the downward portion of the swing.*

Downhill Lie: Use your sand wedge and a standard explosion shot swing. The club should enter the sand two to three inches behind the ball. Play an open stance with the clubface slightly hooded. *Swing down and through the ball* to prevent a 'skulled' shot. This shot will be low, fast, and running.

Uphill Lie: Use a sand wedge and a basic 'explosion' shot swing. The club should enter the sand closer to the ball. Since the clubface digs quickly into the sand, make sure you *keep your weight left and finish with a firm deliberate follow-through.*

There are *three keys* to more effective sand play. *The shot cannot be rushed* and must be played without tension in the forearms and shoulders. *Do not quit at the ball* but finish with a high follow-through. *Practice* until you are comfortable with sand play. The shot is not as difficult as it seems. Pros will take a shot in a bunker anytime to one from the greenside rough.

Buried lie. Use the sand wedge to cut down into the sand. Square up the clubface and play the ball closer the right foot.

Hit two to three inches behind the ball and accentuate the downward portion of the swing.

Play an open stance with the clubface slightly hooded. Swing down and through the ball to prevent a 'skulled' shot.

Downhill lie. Hit two to three inches behind the ball.

Uphill lie. Keep your weight left and finish with a firm, deliberate follow-through. Hit closer to the ball.

44

Uneven Lies

Most rounds of golf will produce abnormal lies. Handling these situations is not that difficult if you approach your shot with a positive mental attitude and adjust your swing accordingly.

Uphill Lies:

A ball struck normally from an uphill lie will fly higher and travel a shorter distance. Be sure to adjust for this when selecting a club.

Take a normal stance, standing perpendicular to the slope. This will assure that you **take the club back parallel to the slope.** The follow-through 'post impact' rises quickly with the slope. To hit the ball cleanly, restrict your backswing a little.

The tendency here is to hook the ball, so aim to the right of the target to compensate.

Downhill Lies:

This is probably the most difficult uneven lie to hit from. The ball will travel farther with less loft. Again, adjust your club selection accordingly. Use a more-lofted club.

Stand perpendicular to the slope and **play the ball back a bit in your stance,** nearer the right foot.

Follow the slope on the backswing and **concentrate on staying down through the impact area.** Watch for excessive head movement. The tendency here is to lift the head and 'top' the shot.

A downhill lie has a tendency to fade or slice, so aim to the left of the target.

Sidehill Lies: (Standing Below the Ball)

When the ball is above your feet, stand more erect than normal, assume a square stance and play the ball in the center of your stance. **Choke down on the club.** Keep your weight more towards your toes.

Restrict your backswing somewhat and try to 'sweep' the ball cleanly from the hillside. *The ball has a tendency to hook, so aim to the right.*

Sidehill Lies: (Standing Above the Ball)

Assume a slightly wider stance than normal and bend more at the knees and waist. Play a 'three-quarter' backswing and **concentrate on staying low** throughout the swing. Don't lift your head. *The ball has a tendency to slice, so aim to the left.*

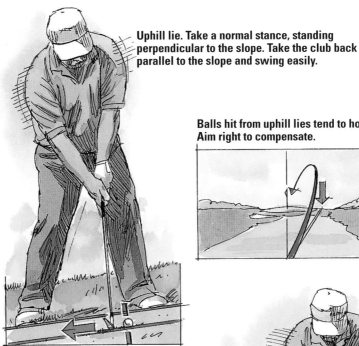

Uphill lie. Take a normal stance, standing perpendicular to the slope. Take the club back parallel to the slope and swing easily.

Balls hit from uphill lies tend to hook. Aim right to compensate.

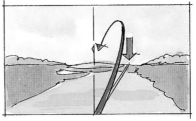

Downhill lies. This the most difficult lie to hit from. Stand perpendicular to the slope and play the ball back in your stance. Follow the slope on the backswing and stay down through the impact zone. Don't lift your head!

Balls hit from a downhill lie tend to fade or slice, so aim to the left to compensate.

Ball above the feet. Choke down on the club. Play for a hook.

Ball below the feet. Bend the knees and waist and stay down through the shot. Play for a slice.

Wet Weather

Playing well in the rain can challenge even the best golfer. ***Developing a positive mental attitude to wet weather golf is probably the most important aspect of posting a decent score.***

In addition to a positive attitude, there are three factors that will influence better rain play, namely, a good grip, balance, and proper club selection.

Proper Grip: When playing in the rain, it is of the utmost importance to maintain a good grip. ***Carry one or two extra dry gloves.*** To prevent slippage, try to keep your grips dry and wipe your hands before every shot. ***Carry two towels,*** one to wipe the clubs, and the other to keep your hands dry. Keep one towel in the rungs of your umbrella to keep it dry.

Balance: To assure good footing in sloppy weather, ***clean your cleats repeatedly*** with a tee or pitch-mark repairer. Plant your feet firmly and swing more 'flatfooted' than normal.

Club Selection: Accept the fact that you will get less distance in wet weather. Compensate by selecting one club more for extra carry.

- **On long fairway shots,** many scratch golfers prefer fairway woods to long irons. The flat bottomed woods give more consistent results in that they are less likely to dig into soggy turf.

- **Conversely, on short approach shots,** wet weather will sometimes cause a 'flier'. The club impact produces less backspin, causing the ball to fly farther than normal. Try hitting one club less to compensate.

- **When near the green,** many low handicappers will chip to the flag for more consistent results. ***A less lofted iron gives a more predictable hit.*** There is less chance of the club digging into the wet turf.

- Others prefer to ***'hit to the flag'*** using a lofted pitch, counting on the ball to 'plug' near the flag. Use whatever works best for you.

Putting: Putts will break less on wet greens. ***Hit the ball more firmly*** and play for less break.

Invest in a plastic bag cover to keep your clubs dry. Keep it in the trunk of the car or in your locker. Always carry an umbrella. The weather can turn quickly during a four hour round.

In wet weather, it is essential to keep your equipment dry. Carry two towels, one to wipe the clubs and the other to keep your hands dry. Keep a plastic bag cover in your locker. They're cheap and make a huge difference in keeping your grips dry.

Assure good footing by cleaning your cleats repeatedly.

When near the green chip to the flag for more consistent results. There's less chance for error with a less-lofted club. Play more aggressively and allow for less roll.

When there is casual water between you and the green, 'hit to the flag' using a lofted pitch and count for the ball to 'plug' near the flag.

46

Allow for putts to break less on wet greens. Hit the ball harder and make sure you get the ball to the hole.

Playing golf in windy conditions calls for definite game adjustments both in club selection as well as in the types of shots played. ***The most important game adjustment is to maintain good tempo and to avoid the temptation to over-power a shot when faced with either a head wind or tailwind.***

Analyze the force and direction of the wind and introduce the following adjustments to improve your scores.

Headwind: The key to maximizing distance when faced with an upwind shot is to try to keep the ball low.

1. On teed shots, ***tee the ball slightly lower*** than normal.

2. ***Play the ball one to two inches farther back in your stance*** to create a lower flight.

3. Above all, ***avoid the temptation to 'smash' the ball*** for extra distance.

4. With fairway shots, drop down one or two clubs and ***swing easy.***

5. ***Play for low approaches to the green.*** Try a punch shot. Position the ball farther back in your stance, near the right foot. Set up with your hands well ahead of the ball and keep the hands ahead on the follow-through. With the punch shot, the hands don't roll over through impact, but keep the clubface square to the target. Use one or two clubs more.

Tailwind: A following or downwind will obviously add distance to your shot.

1. On teed shots, ***tee the ball slightly higher*** than normal.

2. On the fairway, ***use one or two clubs less than normal*** for greater loft and distance.

3. ***Avoid the temptation to 'smash' the ball for extra yardage.*** Swing easy. Slow your tempo.

Crosswind: A crosswind can decrease distance as well as accuracy.

1. Use one more club and ***allow for drift*** by hitting slightly into the wind.

2. ***Tee away from trouble.*** In a left-to-right crosswind (with trouble on the right) tee to the right side of the teeing area and hit away from trouble.

In addition to throwing grass into the air, look to the tree tops and flag to determine wind direction and force.

If you hit fairway woods well, consider hitting your driver into a heavy head wind. If you have a good lie, choke down on the club and swing easy. Practice this one before attempting the shot during a match.

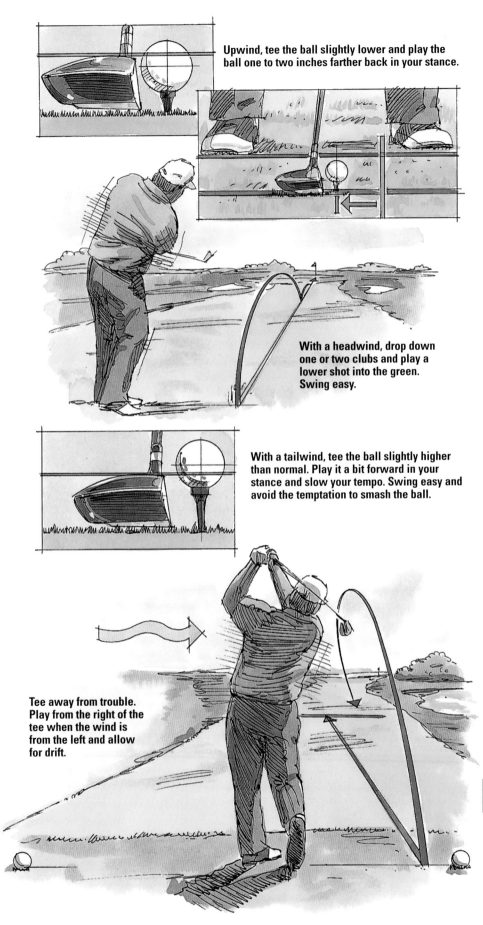

Upwind, tee the ball slightly lower and play the ball one to two inches farther back in your stance.

With a headwind, drop down one or two clubs and play a lower shot into the green. Swing easy.

With a tailwind, tee the ball slightly higher than normal. Play it a bit forward in your stance and slow your tempo. Swing easy and avoid the temptation to smash the ball.

Tee away from trouble. Play from the right of the tee when the wind is from the left and allow for drift.

47

The 18th hole, Melrose,
Daufuskie Island, SC

Club Distance Chart

Touring pros and low handicap amateurs have a good idea of the various yardages they can hit. The next time you are on a practice range, jot down your average distances with all your full shots. Knowing how far you can hit a club takes one element of uncertainty out of an already challenging game.

Club	Men's Average Distance (yds)	Women's Average Distance (yds)	Your Average Distance (yds)
Woods			
Driver	210 and up	180 and up	
Two	200-220	175-185	
Three	190-210	170-180	
Four	180-200	160-170	
Five	170-190	150-160	
Seven	160-180	140-150	
Irons			
Two	180-190	150-160	
Three	170-180	140-150	
Four	160-170	130-140	
Five	150-160	120-130	
Six	140-150	110-120	
Seven	130-140	100-110	
Eight	120-130	90-100	
Nine	110-120	80-90	
Pitching Wedge	100-110	70-80	
Sand Wedge	80-90	50-60	

Golf Etiquette

The very roots of the game of golf are based on proper course etiquette. Golf etiquette covers the game's unwritten rules of conduct and is no less important than the 'official' written rules of the sport.

The fundamental rules of course etiquette involve respect for fellow golfers. This covers consideration for others ahead and behind your group as well as respect for the course itself.

Always observe the following pointers on proper course etiquette.

General:

The game of golf is based on courtesy. Always be courteous to those in your group and to others on the course.

Don't distract fellow competitors by moving, talking, or standing close to a player about to hit a shot.

Do not stand directly behind the ball when a fellow golfer is about to hit on the fairway, and stand away from the line of another's putt when on the green.

Match Priorities on the Course:

1. *Single's matches* (2 golfers) have *first priority* and should be allowed to pass other kinds of matches. During weekend play on busy courses this is sometimes waived since the twosome would continually run into foursomes ahead.

2. A *single golfer* has no standing and has no right to interfere with any type of match play.

3. Any match playing 18 holes has a right to play through any match playing a shorter round.

4. *Slower matches should allow faster matches to play through if the hole ahead is clear. This is a fundamental rule of etiquette that is often overlooked in many areas of the country.*

Through the Green:

Never play a shot unless the players ahead are well out of range. Besides being dangerous, it is impossible to concentrate on playing a good shot when worrying about the players ahead. Always shout 'FORE!' if your shot approaches another golfer.

After hitting from a bunker, always smooth the sand with the rake provided.

Do not delay the game:

While waiting for others to hit, mentally prepare by selecting your club and planning your shot.

Be ready to hit when it's your turn. Do not delay play unnecessarily by working out the exact yardage to the green.

When searching for a lost ball, never delay the group behind you. Wave them through, then wait for the group to get well out of range.

If your foursome is slower than the group behind, **let them through.** Not waving them through spoils both their round (because of slow play ahead) as well as your own (because you are being pushed).

Replace your divots:

This is an obvious courtesy to fellow golfers and helps preserve the course. Also, do not take divots on practice swings from heavy traffic areas such as the teeing ground.

On the green:

Never park a power cart near the green. As well, avoid laying your bag on the putting surface or apron.

Repair your plug marks. As a courtesy to others and the grounds-keeping staff, repair any other plug marks you may see on the green.

The golfer with the nearest ball to the hole usually tends the flagstick. When tending the flag, be careful not to damage the area around the rim of the cup. Try standing a good arm's length away.

Always **replace the flag** properly after putting out.

When your group has putted out, tamp down any **spike marks** left from previous groups.

In the interest of fast play, always **leave the putting green quickly,** as soon as the last putt is holed out. **Don't delay your leaving the green to mark scores or count bets.**

The 7th hole, Arroyo, Pamilla,
Los Cabos, Mexico

Rules Violations Index

Understanding Rules Violations

51

Understanding the rules of golf is essential to the proper enjoyment of the game. The following charts, listed in alphabetical order, serve as a quick reference on some of the more common situations you could encounter on the course. ***The charts are not intended to replace the official rules of golf since many of the situations encountered during a round cannot be simplified in such a format.***

Every golfer should carry The Rules of Golf as jointly published by the United States Golf Association and the Royal and Ancient Golf Club of St. Andrews. This inexpensive publication is available in most pro shops and book stores.

Another excellent publication, officially endorsed by the U.S.G.A., is The New Rules of Golf, written by Tom Watson with Frank Hannigan, published by Random House, New York. The book is fully illustrated and includes a rules quiz that challenges your understanding of the game.

Play by the Rules.

You may think that only novice golfers could benefit from a better understanding of the rules. Think again! At the 1987 San Diego Open, I was disqualified after the fourth round because of a gaffe that had occurred on the fourteenth hole of the previous day's play. My drive came to rest under a small pine tree. I could advance the ball by kneeling under the limbs and swinging from this position. Being the sharp dresser that I am, I dropped a towel on the ground to keep my light blue pants clean.

A television viewer phoned in the next day and asked whether putting a towel down constituted 'building' a stance. The rules officials agreed.

The penalty for 'building a stance' is two strokes. Because I wasn't aware of the violation, I signed a score card that totaled two strokes less than I actually scored. Penalty? Disqualification!

Using the towel cost me second-place prize money, disqualified me from competing for the Vardon trophy that year, and removed any chance to lead a Tour statistics category that would have earned me $25,000.

Needless to say, if you are not sure of a rule, check with your playing partner and read the official U.S.G.A. Rules of Golf until you know them backwards.

The following are examples of some of the rules violations I've seen throughout my career.

Definitions

Stroke (Medal) Play is defined as a competition based on the total **number of strokes taken.** In stroke play, other golfers are called **competitors or fellow-competitors.** The majority of tournaments you watch on television are stroke-play format.

Match Play is defined as a competition based on the **number of holes won.** The golfer you are playing against is called your **opponent.** For example, if I am four holes up with three holes remaining, I win the match.

Ball Playing

Infringement	Penalty	
	Stroke Play	Match Play
Deflecting or Stopping a Moving Ball		
Moving ball is stopped or moved by an outside agency such as an animal, spectator, or fellow competitor in stroke play	No penalty Ball is played where it lies	No penalty Ball is played where it lies
Ball deflects off a tree or rock and strikes player, partner, or his/her equipment	Two strokes When a ball strikes a player during a drop, the ball is re-dropped. No penalty	Loss of hole
Player, partner, or caddie deliberately stops ball from going out of bounds or into a water hazard	Two strokes Possible disqualification by committee	Loss of hole Possible disqualification by committee
Ball is accidentally deflected or stopped by opponent, opponent's caddie, or equipment	Player has the option of replaying the shot or playing the ball where it lies	Player has the option of replaying the shot or playing the ball where it lies
Chip onto the green hits another ball	Ball is played where it comes to rest No penalty Other ball must be replaced in original position	Ball is played where it comes to rest No penalty Other ball must be replaced in original position
Player putting on the green hits another ball on the green	Two strokes	Two strokes

52

Your partner or caddie
Stroke Play – Two stroke penalty
Match Play – Loss of hole

A) Your bag

B) Fellow competitor's or opponent's bag

A) Your bag
Stroke Play – Two stroke penalty
Match Play – Loss of hole

B) Fellow competitor's bag (Stroke Play)
No penalty. Play the ball where it lies.
Opponent's bag (Match Play)
You have the option of immediately replaying
the shot without penalty.

Ball Playing

Infringement	Penalty	
	Stroke Play	Match Play
Hitting the Wrong Ball		
Player hits the wrong ball while playing a match		Loss of Hole
Both players play the wrong ball in match play		First player to hit a wrong ball loses the hole If impossible to determine, the hole is played with the balls exchanged
Player substitutes a new ball on the putting green (unless replacing a damaged ball)	Two strokes, then player must hit the correct ball	Loss of hole
In stroke play, player hits the wrong ball	Two strokes Note: Player then hits the correct ball. Stroke with the wrong ball does not count.	
Player does not correct his or her mistake	Disqualification	

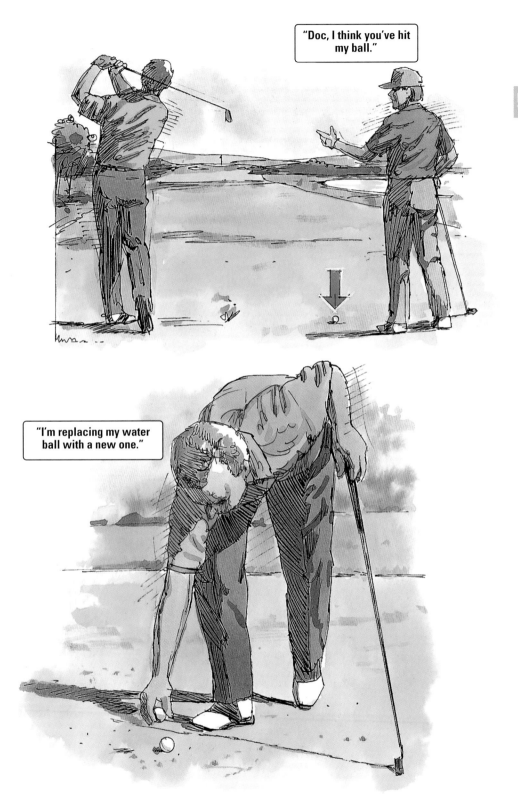

53

Stroke Play – Two strokes, then hit the correct ball
Match Play – Loss of hole
Failure to correct – Disqualification

Infringement	Penalty	
	Stroke Play	Match Play
Moving a Ball at Rest		
Ball is moved by an outside agency, e.g., an animal	No penalty Replace ball	No penalty Replace ball
Ball is moved by player at address	One stroke Replace ball	One stroke Replace ball
Ball in hazard moves after player has taken stance	One stroke Replace ball	One stroke Replace ball
Player, partner, caddie, or equipment moves ball in play	One-stroke penalty Replace ball Except when permitted by the rules 1. when measuring farthest ball from the hole 2. searching for covered ball in a hazard 3. repairing plug mark 4. removing a loose impediment on the green 5. lifting or replacing a ball (under a rule) 6. removing a movable obstruction	One-stroke penalty Replace ball
Ball is moved by opponent (match play) during search		No penalty Replace ball
Ball is moved by opponent, caddie, or opponent's equipment other than during search		Opponent incurs a one-stroke penalty Replace ball
Player's ball is accidentally moved by fellow-competitor, or their caddie in stroke play	No penalty Replace ball	
Player's ball is moved by another ball	No penalty Ball must be replaced	No penalty Ball must be replaced
Player fails to return ball to original position for all of the above conditions	Two strokes	Loss of hole

Ball moved by an animal
No penalty – replace ball

54

Ball moves after being addressed by the player or moves after the player takes his stance in a hazard
Stroke Play – One stroke penalty
Match Play – One stroke penalty

Ball accidentally moved
• **by player in stroke play** – One stroke penalty
• **by player, ball covered in a hazard** – No penalty
• **by fellow competitor (stroke play)** – No penalty
• **by opponent (match play) other than search**
  – One stroke penalty to opponent
• **by opponent (match play) during search** – No penalty

Infringement	Penalty	
	Stroke Play	Match Play
Playing the Ball as It Lies		
Player moves his or her ball away from a divot hole **Player steps immediately behind his or her ball to improve lie** **Player bends tree branches away from swing path**	Two strokes	Loss of hole
Player kicks away rocks to get a more even stance in a hazard or moves an out-of-bounds stake	Two strokes	Loss of hole
Player removes leaves from behind the ball in a hazard	Two strokes	Loss of hole
Player tests the sand with wedge before bunker shot	Two strokes	Loss of hole
	Note: If a player falls into a hazard and grounds a club, no penalty is incurred. It is a violation to ground a club in a hazard.	
Player 'slams' his or her wedge into the sand after failing to get out of a bunker	Two strokes	Loss of hole
Player moves a red or yellow water hazard stake	No penalty	No penalty
	Permitted, but make sure you replace the stake after your shot.	

55

**Player moves a ball from
a divot hole or bare spot**
Stroke Play – Two stroke penalty
Match Play – Loss of hole

**Player steps behind his
ball to improve lie**
Stroke Play – Two stroke penalty
Match Play – Loss of hole

**Player 'rearranges' tree
branches to improve his swing**
Stroke Play – Two stroke penalty
Match Play – Loss of hole

**Player tests the
sand in a bunker**
Stroke Play – Two stroke penalty
Match Play – Loss of hole

Ball Playing

Infringement	Penalty	
	Stroke Play	Match Play
Searching for a Ball/Ball Identification		
Player pulls out tufts of grass and breaks branches while trying to find ball **Player uncovers most of ball buried in a hazard in order to identify it and fails to restore ball to original position**	Two strokes Note: Player is allowed only to move grass or branches carefully without undue disturbance. Improving lie stance or line is not permitted.	Loss of hole Also, if a ball is buried in sand in a bunker, player may play shot since there is no penalty for hitting a wrong ball from a hazard. Player does not have to identify his or her ball before proceeding from a bunker or water hazard.
Player marks and lifts ball on the fairway in order to identify it after telling his or her opponent or fellow competitor of their intention of doing so and allowing competitor to observe procedure **Player fails to follow above procedure** **Player lifts ball in hazard in order to identify it**	No penalty Note: Player may not clean the ball. However, a small amount of mud may be removed if ball cannot be identified by any other means. One stroke One stroke Replace ball in original lie	No penalty Note: Player cannot lift ball in a hazard since there is no penalty for playing a wrong ball from a bunker or water hazard. One stroke One stroke Replace ball in original lie
Player lifts and cleans ball in order to see if it is fit for play	One stroke	One stroke

**Player pulls out tufts
of grass to find her ball**
Stroke Play – Two stroke penalty
Match Play – Loss of hole

56

**Player marks and lifts his
ball resting on the
fairway after telling
opponent of intention**
No penalty

**Player lifts a plugged ball in a
hazard in order to identify it**
Stroke Play – one stroke penalty
Match Play – one stroke penalty

Infringement	Penalty	
	Stroke Play	Match Play
Stroking the Ball		
Player scoops or pushes the ball	Two strokes	Loss of hole
Caddie holds umbrella over golfer during putt	Two strokes	Loss of hole
Player uses a distance device to measure length of shot	Disqualification	Disqualification
Player 'chili-dips' a shot, i.e., hits the ball twice during the same stroke	Stroke counts and one penalty shot is added	Stroke counts and one penalty shot is added
Player hits a moving ball	Two strokes 1. Except if ball falls off a tee 2. Except if the ball is 'chili-dipped' (see above) 3. Except if the ball moves after the player has started backswing 4. Except as defined below	Loss of hole
Player strokes a moving ball in a water hazard	No penalty. However, if player waits for the position of the ball to improve, i.e., allows a fast moving stream to carry the ball closer to the hole, a two-stroke penalty is assessed.	

Player with a restricted backswing 'scoops' the ball
Stroke Play – Two stroke penalty
Match Play – Loss of hole

57

Caddie keeps his player dry during a putt
Stroke Play – Two stroke penalty
Match Play – Loss of hole

Player uses a distance device
Disqualification

Infringement	Penalty	
	Stroke Play	Match Play
Order of Play		
During match play, from the tee, player plays out of turn **Player plays out of turn on the course**		Opponent may immediately ask that stroke be replayed in the correct order without penalty
During stroke play, player A always hits first in order to assist player B	Disqualification for both players	
Player fails to wait for fellow competitors or opponent to play when hitting a second or provisional ball	No penalty if unintentional However, if player A is attempting to assist player B, disqualification for both players	Opponent may immediately ask that stroke be replayed in the correct order without penalty

Infringement	Penalty	
	Stroke Play	Match Play
Teeing Ground		
Player moves tee-marker to improve stance or line of play	Two strokes	Loss of hole
Ball falls off tee when player is addressing it **Player 'whiffs' shot**	No penalty Re-tee Stroke counts, no penalty	No penalty Re-tee Stroke counts, no penalty
Player tees the ball outside the teeing area and hits **Player hits from the wrong tee**	Two strokes Replay shot, not counting the first stroke outside the teeing area	No penalty Opponent may immediately require player to replay shot
Player fails to correct any of the above violations and tees off on the next hole or leaves the putting green on the last hole of the round	Disqualification	

Player hits out of turn.
Players should hit in order.
In match play, your opponent
may immediately ask you to
replay the shot in the correct
order without penalty.

Player moves the
tee marker to improve
stance or line of play
Stroke Play – Two stroke penalty
Match Play – Loss of hole

Player hits ahead of the tee
markers or from the wrong tee
Stroke play – Two stroke penalty.
Player must replay from the correct
location. Original stroke does not
count. Failure to correct violation
means disqualification.
Match play – No penalty but
opponent may ask player to
replay the shot.

Equipment

Infringement	Penalty	
	Stroke Play	Match Play
Clubs		
Using non-conforming clubs	Disqualification	Disqualification
Changing the playing characteristic of a club, i.e., adding lead tape during round	Disqualification	Disqualification
Adding foreign material to club face or ball, i.e., chalk	Disqualification	Disqualification
Playing with more than 14 clubs	Two strokes on each hole played *Max. four strokes*	Loss of hole for each hole played *Max. two holes*
Continuing to play with club(s) declared in excess of max. (14)	Disqualification	Disqualification
Balls		
Using non-conforming ball	Disqualification	Disqualification
Applying foreign material to ball to change playing characteristics	Disqualification	Disqualification
Failure to follow proper procedure in checking for an unfit ball **1. announce intention** **2. mark** **3. lift** **4. examine but do not clean**	One stroke	One stroke
Player fails to rectify	Two strokes	Loss of hole

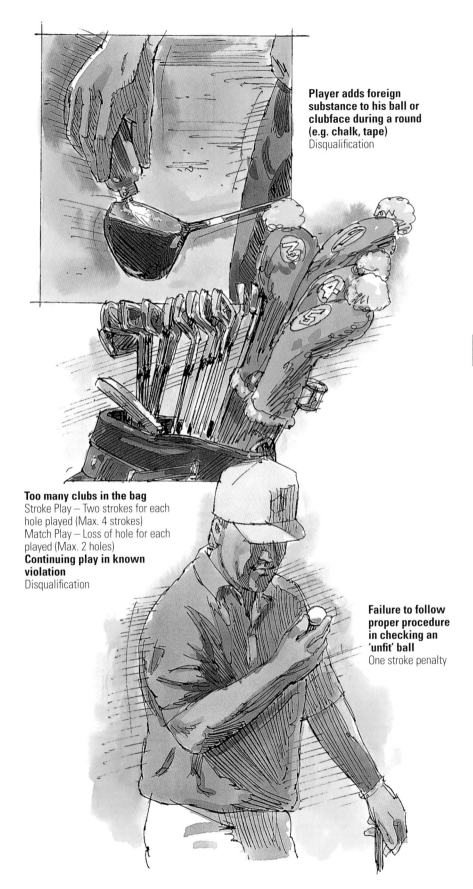

Player adds foreign substance to his ball or clubface during a round (e.g. chalk, tape)
Disqualification

60

Too many clubs in the bag
Stroke Play – Two strokes for each hole played (Max. 4 strokes)
Match Play – Loss of hole for each played (Max. 2 holes)
Continuing play in known violation
Disqualification

Failure to follow proper procedure in checking an 'unfit' ball
One stroke penalty

Player

Infringement	Penalty	
	Stroke Play	Match Play
General Conduct		
Declares a higher handicap than allowed	Disqualification	Disqualification
Arrives late for start	Disqualification Can play with a two stroke penalty as long as his or her group has not played their 2nd shot on the 1st hole.	Disqualification Can play with a two stroke penalty as long as his or her group has not played their 2nd shot on the 1st hole.
Employs more than one caddie	Disqualification	Disqualification
Fails to sign score card	Disqualification	
Signs a score card LOWER than actually taken	Disqualification	
Signs a score card HIGHER than actually taken	Higher score stands	
Causes undue delay	Two strokes	Loss of hole
Repeatedly causes undue delay	Disqualification	Disqualification
Player discontinues play without permission	Disqualification Exceptions: 1) Committee suspends play 2) Danger from lightning 3) Player is seeking decision 4) Sudden illness	Opponents may agree to suspend match play until weather clears (as long as they do not delay a competition)
Failure to return lifted ball to original spot after resumption of play, e.g., after lightning delay	Two strokes	Loss of hole

"I'm not signing the card"
Disqualification

"I'll claim a handicap two strokes higher than my actual one"
Disqualification

Signs a score card lower than actually taken
Disqualification
Signs a score card higher than actually taken
Higher score stands

"...then Walter bought Chrysler warrants when everyone else was bailing out!"

Player causes undue delay
Match Play – Loss of hole
Stroke Play – Two stroke penalty

Infringement	Penalty	
	Stroke Play	Match Play
Advice		
Asking or giving advice other than to partner or caddie	Two strokes Note: Player may ask about the rules or position of the flagstick (public information)	Loss of hole
Player leaves bag or club on line of shot to a blind green or has caddie stand on the line during shot **Caddie or partner touches the line of a putt to assist golfer determine line**	Two strokes Note: Player may have line of play indicated, i.e., approach to a blind green, as long as person indicating the line moves away when shot is played	Loss of hole When on the green, caddie or partner may indicate the line of putt as long they do not touch or mark the green. Caddie must move away from line of putt when stroke is taken
Information as to Strokes Taken		
Player fails to tell competitor that he or she has taken a penalty stroke or gives false information as to the number of strokes taken	No penalty However, player should tell marker as soon as practical that a penalty has been taken	Loss of hole (unless competitor is informed before next stroke)
Practice		
Playing on course the day of competition	Disqualification Note: Rule may be reversed by Committee	Permitted
Playing a practice stroke while playing a hole or between two holes	Two strokes Note: Player may practice chipping or putting on or near last green played or next teeing area as long as play is not delayed In order to practice on a green just played, a U.S.G.A. local rule must be in effect Practice in a hazard is not allowed	Loss of hole

Player asks or gives advice to opponent or fellow competitor
Stroke Play – Two stroke penalty
Match Play – Loss of hole

Player leaves her bag on line to a blind green to help direction
Stroke Play – Two stroke penalty
Match Play – Loss of hole

62
63
64

Player's caddy touches the line of the putt
Stroke Play – Two stroke penalty
Match Play – Loss of hole

The Putting Green

Infringement	Penalty	
	Stroke Play	Match Play
The Putting Green		
Player uses a towel or shoes to clear loose sand and leaves from line of putt	Two Strokes	Loss of Hole
Player taps down spike marks with putter	Two Strokes	Loss of Hole
Caddie touches line of putt or stands behind the hole in a position to indicate the line of the putt	Two Strokes	Loss of Hole
Player stands astride line of putt	Two Strokes	Loss of Hole
Opponent concedes putt but player hits it anyway and misses		Irrelevant (putt is conceded)
Player hits a conceded putt in a four-ball match in order to help his/her partner's line		Partner loses hole
The Flagstick		
Putt from the green strikes the flagstick. This applies whether the flagstick is in the hole or set aside on the green	Two strokes and the ball is played where it has come to rest	Loss of hole

"I'll sweep the sand away from the line!"
Stroke Play – Two stroke penalty
Match Play – Loss of hole

Tapping down spike marks on the putting line
Stroke Play – Two stroke penalty
Match Play – Loss of hole

Putting astride the line
Stroke Play – Two stroke penalty
Match Play – Loss of hole

Putt strikes the flagstick
Stroke Play – Two stroke penalty
Match Play – Loss of hole
(Play the ball where it comes to rest)

Infringement	Penalty	
	Stroke Play	Match Play
Ball (Assisting Play or Interfering)		
Player refuses to lift ball interfering with another player's ball	Two strokes	Loss of hole
Ball (Cleaning)		
Player cleans ball after lifting to determine if it is fit to play	One Stroke	One Stroke
Player cleans ball after lifting to identify	One Stroke Note: Player may clean only enough of the ball to determine identity	One Stroke
Player cleans mud from ball after being asked to lift it because ball interferes with opponent's or fellow-competitor's ball	One stroke Note: In all of the above, the ball may be cleaned if it is on the green	One stroke

Player cleans ball to determine if it is fit to play or after lifting to identify
Stroke Play – One stroke penalty
Match Play – One stroke penalty
Note: Player can only clean enough of the ball to determine identity. Balls on the green can always be cleaned without penalty.

Relief Situations and Procedures

Infringement	Penalty	
	Stroke Play	Match Play
Ball (Dropping, Lifting, or Placing)		
Player lifts ball without marking its position with a coin, ball marker, or similar object	One stroke	One stroke
Player fails to replace ball and mark properly after an improper lift	Two strokes	Loss of hole
Player accidentally moves ball or ball marker in the process of marking and lifting ball	No penalty Marker or ball must be replaced	
Ball hits player while dropping a ball	No penalty Re-drop **Note:** Ball must be dropped in accordance with the rules • stand erect • shoulder height • arm's length	
Player drops ball over shoulder	One stroke See note above	One stroke
Dropped ball moves more than two club-lengths or nearer the hole	No penalty Re-drop Note: Other conditions requiring re-drop include 1. -rolling into a hazard 2. -rolling out of a hazard 3. -rolling onto a green 4. -rolling out-of-bounds 5. -rolling back onto cart path or ground under repair On re-dropping, if any of the above situations occur, the ball is to be placed at the point where the re-dropped ball struck the ground	

(continued on following pages ▶)

Player lifts her ball from the green without marking its position
Stroke Play – One stroke penalty
Match Play – One stroke penalty

Player fails to replace the ball in the correct position
Stroke Play – Two stroke penalty
Match Play – Loss of hole

Ball strikes the player during a drop, moves closer to the hole, or more than 2 club-lengths
No penalty, re-drop
If, on redropping, the same occurs, the ball is placed at the point when the redropped ball struck the ground.

Relief Situations and Procedures

Infringement	Penalty	
	Stroke Play	Match Play
Ball (Dropping, Lifting, or Placing, Cont.)		
Player A's ball touches B's ball on fairway. B is away. Player A marks and replaces nearest original lie not nearer the hole and within one club-length	No penalty Failure to lift, drop, place, or replace ball properly Two strokes	No penalty Failure to lift, drop, place, or replace ball properly Loss of hole
	Note: In a bunker, the original lie of A's ball must be recreated	
Player fails to return to tee or place of last stroke after hitting first ball out of bounds	Two strokes On the tee, second ball may be reteed	Loss of hole Ball that is dropped in a wrong place or not according to the rules can be re-dropped with no penalty
Player plays a wrongly dropped ball or plays a ball dropped from the wrong place	Two strokes	Loss of hole

(continued from the preceding pages ◀)

"I'll just throw the ball 'in-bounds' and take a one stroke penalty."

Stroke Play – Two stroke penalty
Match Play – Loss of hole
If the breach is not corrected before teeing off on the next hole, the player is disqualified in stroke play.

Relief Situations and Procedures

Ball (Embedded)

Definition: A ball is said to be embedded if it comes to rest in its own pitch mark.

Relief: Ball can be lifted, cleaned, and dropped without penalty as close to the original position as possible, not nearer the hole. A player is entitled to relief only if the ball comes to rest on closely mown grass cut to fairway height or less.

Infringement	Penalty	
	Stroke Play	Match Play
Ball (Embedded)		
Player takes relief for embedded ball in the first cut of rough	Two strokes Many clubs have a local rule that relief is given for embedded balls 'through the green'.	Loss of hole
Player claims relief from embedded ball in the bank of a hazard	No relief. Proper procedure is to drop out of the hazard with a one stroke penalty. Or play the ball as it lies.	

"Player lifts embedded ball from rough."

Stroke Play – Two stroke penalty
Match Play – Loss of hole

"My ball's embedded in the creek bed. I get relief."

Stroke Play – Two stroke penalty
Match Play – Loss of hole

69

Ball (Lost or Out of Bounds/Provisional Ball)

Definition: A ball is considered **lost** if it cannot be found after a five minute search. Excluded from this definition are balls lost in casual water, water hazards, or lost in immovable obstructions such as a pile of brush waiting to be carted away from the course.

A ball is considered lost if the player declares it so and puts a 'second' ball into play.

To speed play, a player is allowed to hit a **'provisional' ball** to avoid having to return to the tee should a ball not be found after a five minute search. The player **must** declare that a 'provisional' ball is in play. Otherwise, the first is considered lost and the second ball is in play.

The player is allowed to hit the provisional ball up to the point where the first is likely to be. If the player hits the provisional beyond that point, it automatically becomes the ball in play.

Penalty for a lost ball is one stroke plus distance.

In other words, if a ball is hit out of bounds or lost off the tee, the player hits his or her third stroke from the tee box.

If you do not follow this procedure, the penalty is two strokes in stroke play and loss of hole in match play.

Infringement	Penalty	
	Stroke Play	Match Play
Ball (Lost or Out of Bounds/Provisional Ball)		
Player fails to declare that he or she is playing a provisional ball	Provisional ball is in play automatically. Saying "I'll reload" or "I'll hit a second" puts the second ball in play automatically	
Player hits provisional ball past the point where the first ball is likely to be	Provisional ball is in play	
Caddie finds original ball in unplayable position before provisional ball is hit again (as above)	Provisional ball must be abandoned. If it is not, Two-stroke penalty	Provisional ball must be abandoned If it is not, Loss of hole
Player hits original ball into a water hazard and declares a provisional ball in play	If the first shot clearly went into the hazard, the second ball is automatically in play. Hitting a second from the tee is one option available to a golfer for hitting into a water hazard.	**Note:** A provisional ball cannot be played if the original clearly went into the water hazard. Golfer should proceed under options governing water hazards.

You are limited to a five minute search for a lost ball. Allow groups behind to play through.
Always hit a 'provisional' ball off the tee to speed play if you think your ball is lost.

Once a provisional ball is hit past the point where the original ball is likely to be, the provisional ball is in play.
Player can declare the original ball lost without waiting for a five minute search.

70

Ball (Unplayable)

Definition: A ball can be declared unplayable at any place on the course, excluding water hazards.

Penalty under this rule is one stroke

Relief

Player has three options when declaring an unplayable ball, namely,

1. Stroke and distance
2. Two club-lengths from where the ball lies, not nearer the hole (not two club-lengths from the nearest point of relief)
3. Drop back along the line where the ball lay and the hole. If the ball is in a bunker, the ball must remain in the hazard

The general rule when taking a drop is that a player is allowed two club-length relief if a penalty is involved and one club-length relief when no penalty has occurred.

Infringement	Penalty	
	Stroke Play	Match Play
Ball (Unplayable)		
Player carries the ball from the bushes and declares an unplayable lie	Two-stroke penalty	Loss of hole
	Limit is two club-lengths from where the original lay	
Player declares an unplayable lie in a water hazard	This option is not available.	This option is not available.
	If player drops in a water hazard, two-stroke penalty	If player drops in a water hazard, loss of hole

Player carries the ball from deep rough, drops on the fairway, and declares a one stroke penalty. Not permitted.
Note:
Player is limited to three options
1. Two club lengths from the original point where the ball lay, not nearer the hole.
2. Stroke and distance
3. Back along a line from where the ball lay and the hole

Player declares an unplayable lie in a hazard Not permitted. If done,
Stroke Play – Two stroke penalty
Match Play – Loss of hole

Ground Under Repair

Definition: Ground under repair is defined as any part of the course that has been marked by the committee or groundskeeper as such. Usually the area is marked by lines sprayed on the ground or stakes. Also included under this definition are cuttings and tree branches, etc. that are to be removed by the grounds-keeping staff. Small amounts of cut grass abandoned on the course are not defined as ground under repair.

Relief: Same as casual water

Infringement	Penalty	
	Stroke Play	Match Play
Ground Under Repair		
Player takes an abnormally wide stance to claim relief from ground under repair	No relief Option is to take an unplayable lie (one-stroke penalty)	
Player plays from G.U.R.	Permitted unless forbidden by a local rule	

Player takes an abnormally wide stance to get relief from ground under repair.

No relief. If you want a better lie, you can take an unplayable lie with a one stroke penalty.

Player has the option of playing the ball in ground under repair if the lie is good. *(However, the committee has the right to forbid play in an area of ground under repair to protect new sod, etc.)*

72

Relief Situations and Procedures

Loose Impediments

Definition: Loose impediments are defined as natural objects that are not embedded, fixed, or growing and include such things as leaves, pine cones, twigs, sticks, and worms and their casts .

Infringement	Penalty	
	Stroke Play	Match Play
Loose Impediments		
Through the green, the player moves his or her ball while clearing loose impediments from near the ball	One stroke	One stroke
In a bunker, player moves twigs from behind the ball	Two strokes	Loss of hole
	Note: Loose impediments cannot be moved in a bunker. However, man-made objects, e.g., rakes, cups, cigar butts, etc. can be moved	
On putting surface player accidentally moves marker or ball while brushing away loose sand	No penalty Replace marker or ball **Note:** On the green, sand and loose soil are loose impediments (but not in the fairway or rough)	

Player moves his ball while clearing a twig from near the ball
Stroke Play – One stroke penalty
Match Play – One stroke penalty

Player removes leaves from behind her ball in a bunker
Stroke Play – Two stroke penalty
Match Play – Loss of hole

73

Immovable Obstructions

Definition: These are defined as **artificial objects** that cannot be easily moved. Examples include cart paths, curbs, stone walls, construction equipment, tractors, grass cutters, washrooms, fixed ball washers, and sprinkler heads.

Excluded from the definition are fences, walls, stakes, etc. defining out-of-bounds.

Relief: Through the green, player is allowed to drop within one club-length where there is no interference, not nearer the hole if obstruction interferes with stance or intended swing.

In a hazard, there is no relief from obstructions such as bridges, pipes, etc.

On the green, player gets relief along the intended line of putt. Player places the ball at the nearest point of relief, not nearer the hole.

Infringement	Penalty	
	Stroke Play	Match Play
Immovable Obstructions		
Player attempts to drop from a cart path to a position farther away than the nearest point of relief (as defined)	Not permitted. This is a common rules violation. The drop must be the **nearest point of relief,** not nearer the hole. There is no option as to what side of the path the player can take relief. Player has the option of playing from the path if relief would put the ball in a more difficult position.	
After drop, player still stands on path	Two strokes	Loss of Hole
Player takes an abnormally wide stance in order to stand on a sprinkler head and claim relief	Two strokes	Loss of Hole
Player moves ball away from boundary stake or fence and claims relief	No relief. Player may claim an unplayable lie under a penalty of one stroke. Move away two club-lengths no nearer the hole.	
Player swings away from the hole in order to claim interference	Not permitted	
Player in water hazard claims interference from a bridge	No relief from immovable obstructions in a hazard	

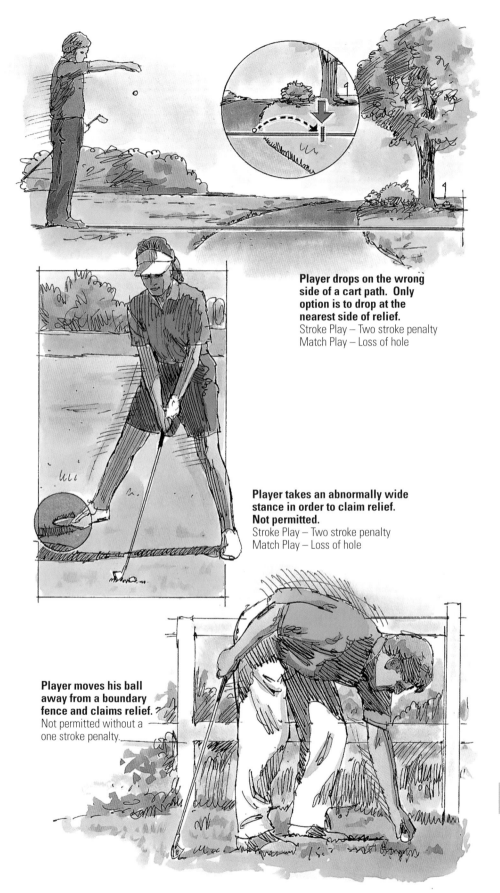

Player drops on the wrong side of a cart path. Only option is to drop at the nearest side of relief.
Stroke Play – Two stroke penalty
Match Play – Loss of hole

Player takes an abnormally wide stance in order to claim relief. Not permitted.
Stroke Play – Two stroke penalty
Match Play – Loss of hole

Player moves his ball away from a boundary fence and claims relief.
Not permitted without a one stroke penalty.

74

Relief Situations and Procedures

Movable Obstructions

Definition: Movable obstructions are defined as artificial objects such as benches, hoses, ball cleaners (not fixed) that can be moved with little difficulty.

Interference occurs when an obstruction prevents a normal stance and swing. **Line-of-sight to the hole is not interference as defined by the rules of golf.**

Relief: Ball is lifted, and the obstruction removed. Drop as near as possible to the ball's original position, no nearer the hole.

Infringement	Penalty	
	Stroke Play	Match Play
Movable Obstructions		
Ball accidentally moves while player is removing hose from immediately in front of the player's ball	No penalty Replace ball	No penalty Replace ball
Player removes an 'out-of-bounds' stake because it interferes with his/her swing	Two strokes	Loss of hole
Ball comes to rest in a small coiled hose left in the rough. Player lifts and drops away from the hose	**Improper procedure** Ball should be lifted and the hose removed. Ball is then dropped as close as possible to where it originally lay. If the hose was left on the green, the ball is placed on the green, not dropped. Ball may be cleaned when lifted in this situation.	
Player moves a red or yellow water hazard stake	No penalty	No penalty
	Permitted, but make sure you replace the stake after your shot.	

Movable obstructions interfere with stance or swing and include hoses, light benches, non-fixed ball cleaners.
If the ball comes to rest on the base of a washer, on a hose, or in a basket, remove the obstruction and drop nearest the original position.

Player removes an out of bounds stake interfering with his swing.
Stroke Play – Two stroke penalty
Match Play – Loss of hole

Casual Water

Definition: Casual water is defined as any temporary accumulation of water visible before or after a player has taken his or her stance. Water in a water hazard is not defined as casual water.

Dew and frost are not defined as casual water.

Ice or snow can be treated as casual water or loose impediments at the player's option.

Relief: Through the green, player is entitled to a **free drop within one club-length** of the nearest point of relief, no nearer the hole.

On the green, player is entitled to lift and place the ball as to avoid the water, not nearer the hole. Player is entitled to relief if casual water is on the intended line of the putt.

In a bunker, player is entitled to drop the ball within one club-length of the nearest point of relief, no nearer the hole, but must remain within the bunker.

On penalty of one stroke, player can drop behind the bunker if the drop is on an extended line from where the original ball lay and the hole.

Infringement	Penalty	
	Stroke Play	Match Play
Casual Water		
Player takes an abnormally wide stance to claim relief from casual water	No relief Option is to take an unplayable lie (one-stroke penalty)	
Player drops behind the bunker, where casual water has accumulated	Player is allowed this option with a one-stroke penalty as long as the ball is dropped on the line between where the original came to rest and the hole	
Ball is lost in a water filled bunker or casual water on the course	If there is reasonable evidence that the ball is indeed in the casual water, drop another ball without penalty However, if there is no evidence that ball is in the casual water, then the ball must be treated as lost (See ball lost)	
Casual water between ball on apron of the green and the hole	No relief	
Player moves the ball more than one club-length from nearest point of relief	Two stokes	Loss of hole

"My ball disappeared in the puddle here!"

No penalty

Player takes an abnormally wide stance in order to claim relief. **Not permitted.**
Stroke Play – Two stroke penalty
Match Play – Loss of hole

"I'll drop in the bunker behind the water."

No penalty

Player has the option of dropping behind the bunker. One stroke penalty

Water Hazards

Definition: Water hazards are defined as any pond, lake, ditch, river, etc., designated as such by the club. These can include dry river beds and ditches. Water hazards are defined by yellow stakes or lines.

Lateral water hazards are designated by red stakes or lines. These are defined as lateral because it is impractical to drop behind them.

Relief: Player has **five options** after hitting into a water hazard.

1. Play the ball as it lies. (no penalty)
2. Replay last shot from original position, and add one penalty stroke.
3. Drop behind the hazard. Add one penalty stroke. The drop must be taken on a line defined by the hole and the point where the original ball crossed the margin of the hazard.
4. Player has two additional options when the ball is hit into a lateral hazard. Drop within two club-lengths from the point where the ball crossed the margin of the hazard, not nearer the hole.
5. The player can also drop on the opposite side of the hazard at a point equidistant from the hole, not nearer the hole.

Infringement	Penalty	
	Stroke Play	Match Play
Water Hazards		
Player hits a blind shot to the green and claims ball is lost in pond	Ball is deemed lost. There must be reasonable evidence the ball did, indeed, enter the hazard.	Same as stroke play
Player hits into regular water hazard and drops at a position other than where the ball entered the hazard	Illegal drop Two-stroke penalty	Illegal drop Loss of hole
	The rule allows you the option of dropping on a line defined by the point where your ball entered the hazard and the hole. A common violation is to move the ball away from the line and drop in a more 'convenient' position.	
Player claims relief from embedded ball in the bank of a hazard	No relief	
Ball moves after player has taken his/her stance in a hazard	One-stroke penalty. Play the ball as it lies.	
Player hits a ball onto a green and spins it back into a regular water hazard (yellow stakes). Player drops on the 'greenside' of the pond.	Illegal drop Two-stroke penalty	Illegal drop Loss of hole
	Player has dropped 'closer' to the hole	

Water hazards
Regular water hazard (Yellow stakes)
Three options
1. Play ball as it lies
2. Replay last shot
3. Drop behind the hazard on a line defined
   from the point of entry and the hole
Penalty- one stroke

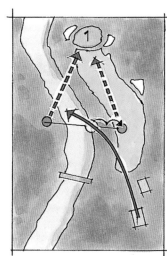

Lateral water hazard (Red stakes)
Same as above
Plus, option of dropping within two club lengths of the point of entry, not nearer the hole.

Player can drop on the opposite bank, at a point equidistant from the hole. Again, drop within two club lengths.

Scores and Practice Priorities

After every round, try summarizing your game using the following criteria. Use up arrows (↑) if you were happy with the results, a side arrow (↔) if the results were so-so, and a down arrow (↓) if this part of your game was unsatisfactory. Don't be too hard on yourself!

Develop a practice routine that works on the specific parts of your game that need improvement.

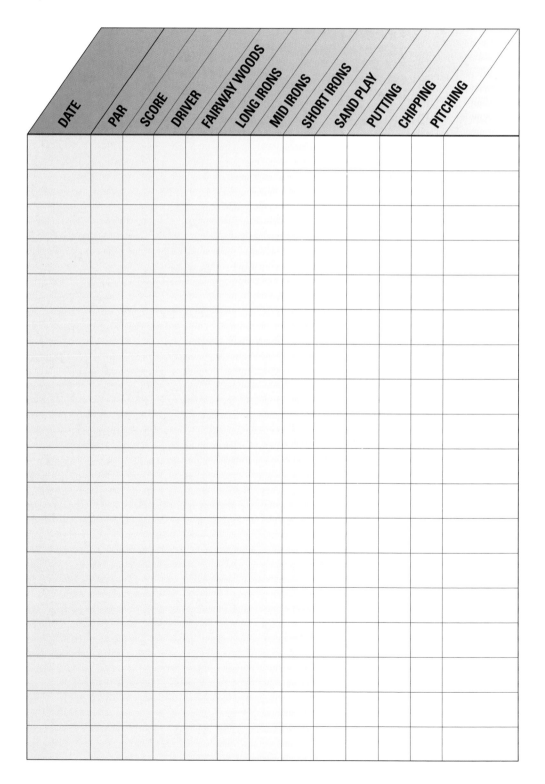

DATE	PAR	SCORE	DRIVER	FAIRWAY WOODS	LONG IRONS	MID IRONS	SHORT IRONS	SAND PLAY	PUTTING	CHIPPING	PITCHING

Develop good practice habits. From the summaries on the previous page, allocate practice time to work on each weakness. Indicate the percentage of time spent on each area of your game.

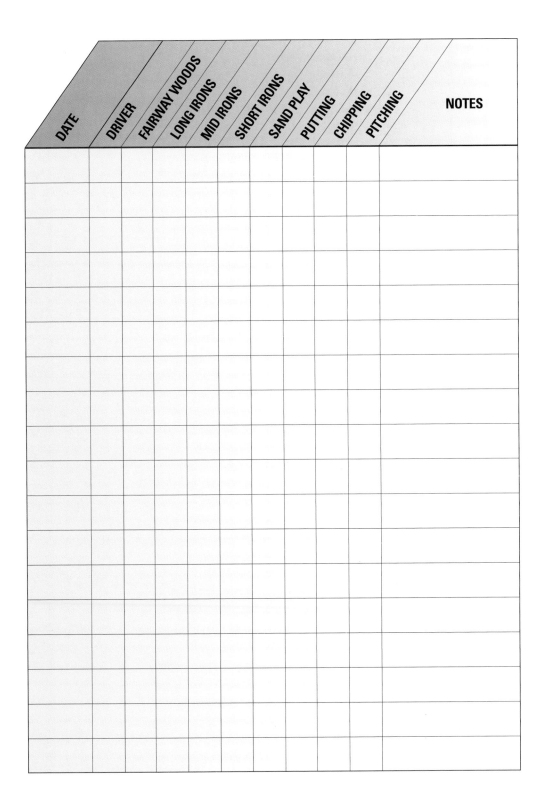

DATE	DRIVER	FAIRWAY WOODS	LONG IRONS	MID IRONS	SHORT IRONS	SAND PLAY	PUTTING	CHIPPING	PITCHING	NOTES

Scores and Practice Priorities

After every round, try summarizing your game using the following criteria. Use up arrows (↑) if you were happy with the results, a side arrow (↔) if the results were so-so, and a down arrow (↓) if this part of your game was unsatisfactory. Don't be too hard on yourself!

Develop a practice routine that works on the specific parts of your game that need improvement.

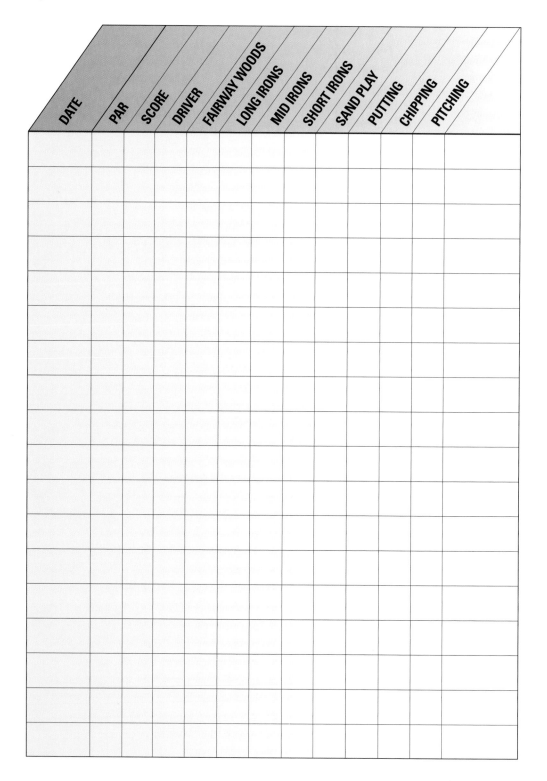

Develop good practice habits. From the summaries on the previous page, allocate practice time to work on each weakness. Indicate the percentage of time spent on each area of your game.

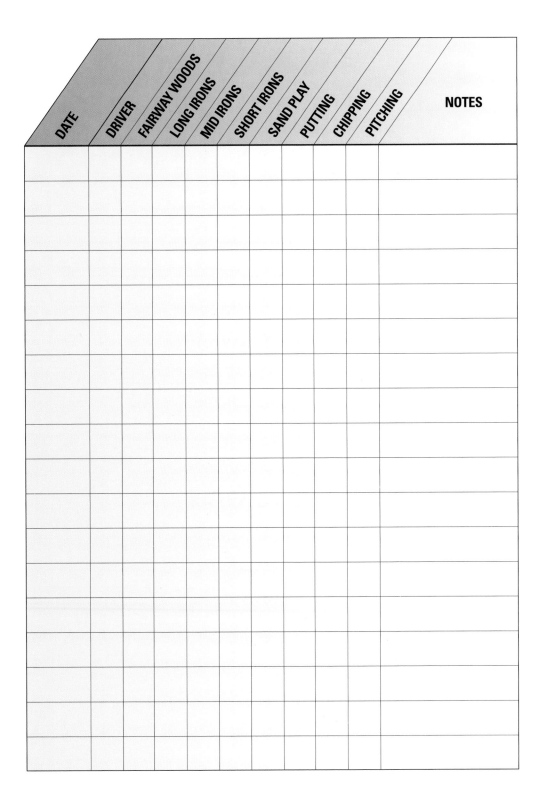

DATE	DRIVER	FAIRWAY WOODS	LONG IRONS	MID IRONS	SHORT IRONS	SAND PLAY	PUTTING	CHIPPING	PITCHING	NOTES